STEEPLECHASING

STEEPLECHASING

A Celebration of 250 Years
1752-2002

Anne Holland

LITTLE, BROWN AND COMPANY
BOSTON • NEW YORK • LONDON

A Little, Brown Book

First published in 2001 by Little, Brown and Company (UK).

Text by Anne Holland (c) copyright 2001

A CIP catalogue record for this book is available from the British Library.

ISBN 0-316-85773 -4

Designed by Wilson Design Associates
Printed and bound in Italy

Little, Brown and Company (UK)
Brettenham House, Lancaster Place,
London WC2E 7EN

Page 2: The statue of Dawn Run and Jonjo O'Neill at Cheltenham Racecourse
Page 7: Jonjo O'Neill
Page 9: Limestone Lad, Shane McGovern up, in the Stayers Hurdle, Cheltenham, 2000

Contents

Acknowledgements

My grateful thanks go to the following, without whom this celebration of steeplechasing could not have been written, and especially to Jonjo O'Neill for kindly contributing the foreword in spite of his being in the middle of his move south at the time. My sincere apologies go to the many more whose stories deserve to lie between these pages. I hope they will view the whole as a broad brush painting typical scenes on the huge canvas that makes up the heroic and historic sport of steeplechasing.

Aintree: Dickon White

Toby Balding

Nick and Belinda Boyd

Judy Bradley

Tommy Carberry

Cheltenham: Peter McNiele

Michael Dickinson

Jim Dreaper

Georgie Ellis

Johnny Francome

Serena Geake

Josh Gifford

Konrad Goess-Saurau

Sirrell Griffiths

Richard Guest

Andrew Gunther

Tom Helme

Nicky Henderson

Injured Jockeys' Fund

Little, Brown: Julia, Arianne, Rachel, Alan

Norman Mason

Stan Mellor

Ginger McCain

Maryland Hunt Cup: William Gallo

Willie O'Brien

Rhona Oliver

Jonjo O'Neill

Sir Peter O'Sullevan

Sue Parrish

Martin Pipe

John and Terry Selby

Tim Richards

Hugh Thomas

Ted Walsh

Weatherbys: Gary Bivens

Weatherbys Ireland: Evan Arkwright

Mary Wilson

Wilson Design Associates: Steve, Mike

Foreword by Jonjo O'Neill

I know speed kills. But it is the speed of the horses that gives me the buzz; riding them or watching them at full stretch on the gallops or on the racecourse is the fix I still enjoy. Speed is my adrenaline pump. I have always felt that if there is no danger, there is no sport or fun, and that means no steeplechasing. I suppose it is a question of knowing how far we can go when we push ourselves and our horses to the limit. From my earliest days in the saddle, the thrill was the chase with the dashing Duhallows across the hunting country of County Cork in Ireland. Those childhood memories will never dim. Around the local villages of Buttevant and Doneraile, along the banks of the Awbeg and the Blackwater, is where steeplechasing started two-and-a-half centuries ago and where my riding began. Those exhilarating hours spent with the Duhallows provided me with my happiest days on horseback.

Wearing a pair of wellies and flat cap, I weighted four stone and must have been like a fly on the back of my pony, Dolly, who was the most wonderful hunter, even from the day of her first meet at the age of sixteen months, hurling over ditches, fences and hedges. I couldn't believe there could be such a kick.

The best hunting in the world and I never paid a penny for it, just stayed friendly with the huntsmen Harry Clayton and Tommy Kavanagh who looked after me. Dolly did her bit as well, keeping me right up there in the van. Although I wasn't aware of it at the time, the thrills and spills with the Duhallows was the launch pad for many exciting years in the saddle as a jockey. But now, would you believe, I don't miss the race riding.

As a jockey you get on and off your horse and that's basically where the job ends. There is so much more involvement with the horses when you are training. The team effort of your staff; choosing the right lad to ride the right horse; finding the right race on the right track on the right ground in the hands of the right jockey. And that's just part of it. I love training and being involved in the whole scene.

Steeplechasing: A Celebration of 250 Years introduces the reader to so many giants of the jumping world, from Vincent O'Brien, who started life in the Duhallow country near Buttevant and Doneraile, to Fulke Walwyn and Fred Winter; from the mighty Arkle and L'Escargot, to my own heroine Dawn Run: men and horses whose achievements tell the story of steeplechasing. There is no hidden mystery to the sport. Just a magic which is like a never-ending magnet. I have always felt it a privilege to be involved.

Jonjo O'Neill, 2001

Introduction

The spring of 2001 that had promised so much in National Hunt racing was nearly wiped out by a Third World disease that had not been seen in the United Kingdom for decades. Foot-and-mouth arrived like a bolt out of the blue, with no warning, no premonition, nor any reason to suspect. Its rampages caused devastation in the countryside.

For National Hunt racing it meant no Cheltenham Festival and all racing in Ireland was halted until late April. The Irish Grand National was postponed until early May; the pearl of Punchestown was lost due to ground problems caused by drainage work. Fairyhouse put on an alternative to Punchestown and in England Sandown substituted alternative Cheltenham Festival races. Brave efforts, with an especially memorable 'Queen Mother', but we will never know for sure who would have won the races lost from the sport's two prime festivals.

As it ended its first quarter millennium, National Hunt racing was knocked but refused to fall. Somehow Aintree survived. And no matter how badly the sport was affected, hopes dashed, dreams shattered, our thoughts still went out to the devastated livestock farmers, many of whom had lost flocks or herds that had taken generations to build up. We still had our horses. Istabraq's attempt at a unique fourth Champion Hurdle was thwarted, but he lives to fight another day.

The exploits of the equine and human characters that unfold on the following pages portray scenes from the first 250 years of steeplechasing and celebrate a truly heroic sport.

PART ONE

The Races

1

Little Polveir, ridden by Jimmy Frost, leads at the last jump of the 1989 Grand National

The 2001 Grand National

All the drama, heroics and horsemanship – humour even – that have epitomised the sport of steeplechasing for 250 years were crammed into the 11 minutes it took to run the 2001 Grand National. Run in pouring rain on ever deepening ground, it illustrated more than anything that the Corinthian spirit is still alive and well, that man and horse can rise together in adversity.

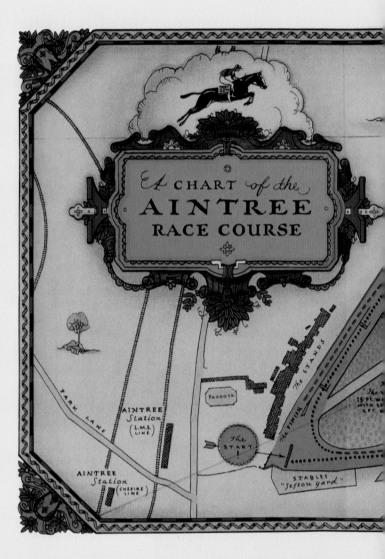

Courage and camaraderie were evident as the forty horses and riders lined up for the awesome race at Aintree, Liverpool, on 7 April 2001. Owners, trainers, organisers and sponsors had shown bravery, too, and an understanding public saluted them all. Only a small section of sanitised Press corps, most of whom have never ridden in a race, let alone the world's greatest steeplechase, allowed vitriol to pour from their pens, condemning the running in atrocious conditions, one calling the decision 'gutless and witless'. Their views were not shared by those riders past and present who also write, for they know steeplechasing is all about risk and danger and,

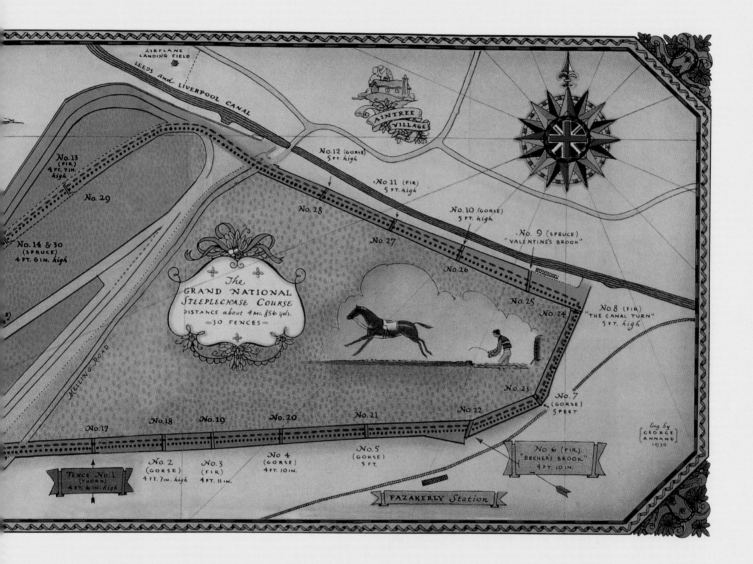

ABOVE: *An early map of the course at Aintree*

while much has been done to reduce it, never can it be eliminated entirely. As it was succinctly put, one might as well ban climbing the Matterhorn because it is too steep – or run a 1½-mile race on the all-weather surface at Lingfield and call it the Grand National.

The one certainty about the Grand National, which once again lived up to its first winner's name, Lottery, is that it never fails to produce a fairy-tale result, and 2001 was no exception. The winner, Red Marauder, was a renowned poor jumper who had spent years at a time off the course with ailments; aided by his jockey, he rose to the occasion in epic fashion. His owner and

permit trainer, Norman Mason, had worked his way from night-club bouncer to owner of a string of leisure establishments. His rider and assistant trainer, Richard Guest, had quit racing in disgust after an altercation with officials – only to come back and show the world what a great and caring horseman he is. Even Red Marauder's name was adopted because red is considered lucky by the Chinese. Norman Mason, hoping it would prove the same for him, has prefixed many of his horses' names with Red. By coincidence, 2001 saw the race covered live in China for the first time. Although it may have been overlooked before his 33–1 victory, Red Marauder was bred to win a National. He was descended from the 1903 winner, Drumcree, and was the great-grandson of Tiberina, the late Edward Courage's mare whose full sister, Tiberetta, was placed three times, and a nephew of Spanish Steps, twice placed in the great race.

In a desperate spring for both British and Irish racing, Aintree was lucky to go ahead at all. The wonderful Cheltenham Festival had already been lost to the ravages of foot-and-mouth disease, and Ireland's pearl, Punchestown, was deemed unfit due to mole drain damage. When the heavens opened and poured their contents on to Liverpool, fate did indeed seem to be doing its direst. The rain did not deter scantily clad 'Liverbirds' from sloshing their way in open-toed sandals, their pale pink and lilac outfits revealing bosoms and arms in near equal proportions.

As pre-race punters looked for mudlarks, it was Welsh Grand National winner, Edmond, who became many people's choice, along with Moral Support, while an old-fashioned plunge brought Inis Cara's price tumbling from 66–1 to joint 10–1 favourite with them. Top weight Beau started at 12–1; he will have gone into many people's notebooks as the likely winner for 2002. Mely Moss, having his first run since finishing second in the race twelve months before, was also well backed.

Dick Saunders, the National's oldest winning jockey when triumphant on Grittar in 1982, is now a steward at Aintree. It was he who gave the traditional pre-race advice to 'hunt round on the first circuit', admonishing jockeys not to go too fast. For once, the advice was heeded, but from the very first fence there were falls, which had little to do with the ground and nothing to do with weariness.

Starter Simon Morant got them off without delay. Would record-breaking champion jockey Tony McCoy on board Blowing Wind complete the race for the first time? Could the previous year's winner, Papillon, be the first dual winner since Red Rum in the 1970s? Might Martin Pipe produce something unimaginable from his incredible bag with his unprecedented ten runners, 25 per cent of the field?

The only certain prospect was that not many would complete. That a quarter of the field would be taken out in one

LEFT: *A triumphant Richard Guest celebrates his victory on Red Marauder*

swipe by a loose horse at the first Canal Turn, or that the whole field would have been decimated to single figures before setting out on the second circuit, could surely not have been foreseen by the most clairvoyant.

The Canal Turn is the eighth fence. All seven fences before had seen fallers: two came down at the first, three at the second and three at the third, significantly including a horse called Paddy's Return. The two at the fourth included the gambled-on Inis Cara; one went at the fifth; two at the sixth, Becher's Brook; and one at the seventh. Less than a quarter of the obstacles had been tackled and fourteen horses were out; Martin Pipe was down to four runners.

Up front, those remaining approached the Canal Turn headed by majestic Beau, who had taken to the fences like the proverbial duck to water and was giving Carl Llewellyn, already twice a victor with Party Politics (1992) and Earth Summit (1998), a dream ride, closely attended by Edmond. Close, too, were Smarty and Blowing Wind, and joining them was the 2000 winner, Papillon. Little Noble Lord was not far away, along with Moondigua, Unsinkable Boxer and Listen Timmy. There, on the inside, was Red Marauder.

As for the remainder, fate was about to intervene: running loose on the wide outside and apparently well out of harm's way was the blinkered Paddy's Return. Suddenly, for no apparent reason, he veered left-handed, running sharply across the front of the fence, causing virtually all the other horses to collapse like a pack of cards.

For the hundreds of thousands of viewers who remembered the 1967 race, it was a case of déjà vu. Whereas then the loose horse had caused havoc at the head of the field, leaving just one back marker, Foinavon, to pop over at the first attempt, at least this time a few cleared the fence ahead of the trouble-maker. Nevertheless, ten were knocked out, making a total of twenty-four runners brought to grief when less than a third of the fences had been jumped. Red Marauder missed the trouble by a whisker – the last horse to do so.

Just behind him, Warren Marston was knocked off

ABOVE: *Heavy rain could not deter the scantily-clad 'liverbirds'*

Amberleigh House, one of two runners trained by 'Mr Red Rum', Ginger McCain. Various other horses landed on different parts of his anatomy, and a horse called Village King fell on top of him, pinning his head beneath the horse's ample hindquarters. It was a terrifying position, but within seconds the fallen horse's jockey, Jim Culloty, mindless of any danger to himself, dashed across to his stricken colleague and, without a thought for flying horses or flailing hooves, grabbed hold of Warren's legs and literally pulled him clear. Three days later, Warren Marston was race-riding again; such is the bravery of steeple-chase jockeys, to say nothing of the bond between them.

The others to be knocked out of contention at this fence included Djeddah, thereby denying his sporting French trainer, François Doumen, and his jockey son Thierry a treble, following hurdler Bilboa and chaser First Gold's victories earlier in the meeting. It was the end, too, for Moral Support, General Wolfe, Mely Moss, You're Agoodun, Feels Like Gold, Dark Stranger and Lance Armstrong, who remounted and continued.

ABOVE: *The mêlée at the 1967 Grand National*

The Fates were not finished yet. The next few fences brought a splattering of falls, but another to prove significant came at the Chair, the 15th, where Edmond lacked enough momentum to clear the biggest fence. Blinkered, like Paddy's Return, he continued loose. As the few remaining runners headed out on to the final circuit, Beau made such a mistake two fences later, at the 17th, that the reins were snatched out of Carl Llewellyn's hands and tossed over one side of the horse's head. The intrepid jockey was left with no means of either steering or braking. He could be seen desperately trying to retrieve the reins and at one time half succeeded, but his attempt left the reins flapping against the horse's eye. Somehow the gallant pair jumped two more fences and missed the next trouble. In front of the 19th, the loose Edmond took it into his head to cannon into other horses, spelling the end for brave Brave Highlander (running in his

fourth National in Aldaniti colours), poor Lance Armstrong, Blowing Wind and Papillon. Beau and Carl could manage only one more fence without reins, and at the 20th they parted company; here, Unsinkable Boxer also called it a day. Incredibly, that left just two horses in the race, Smarty and Red Marauder, with a third of the race to run. The thought occurred: would there be any finishers at all?

Poor Carl tried desperately to hold on to Beau's reins and, when he finally had to let go, could be seen running down the course in vain pursuit. A few moments later, the race still in progress, Beau's trainer, Nigel Twiston-Davies, watching in the stands, received a call on his mobile telephone.

'How much money is there for fifth place?' an astounded Nigel heard Carl ask. The jockey, making use of twenty-first century technology, had borrowed the phone from the person who had caught Beau.

'£12,000,' came the reply, and 'decide for yourself what to do.'

Beau had a small cut, so Carl, younger by a fortnight than the current senior jockey, Richard Guest, called it a day.

Back at the 19th, again courtesy of modern technology, this time the big screen displaying the action, Tony McCoy and Ruby Walsh sized up the situation and, showing a blend of maturity and adventurism, remounted to continue side by side, chatting, enjoying themselves, going just fast enough for their horses to clear the big fences safely. One only has to look at the picture of Tony's face to see how much he relished the challenge that was to earn him a prize in the race after all.

Meanwhile, fully two fences ahead of them, Smarty and his rider, Timmy Murphy, and Richard Guest on Red Marauder were also playing it safe, racing together, giving each horse the extra encouragement needed for tackling those big fences. Incredibly, another loose horse cut a narrow zigzag between them as they approached a fence. For a moment it looked as though both would be zapped. Instead, they galloped on, the only two to go the whole slog, and therefore the only ones to

become really tired. By keeping together, they helped each other last out. With the ground being as freshly wet as it was, it was easier for the horses than if it had begun to dry out, when it would have resembled glue. But no one denies it was a mammoth, gruelling task – so is climbing the Matterhorn!

Red Marauder had fallen the previous year at only the sixth fence, Becher's Brook, and his consummate horseman, Richard Guest, the regular rider at exercise of the great Derby winner Shergar when a schoolboy, was determined it shouldn't happen again. Richard's spell with trainer Sue Smith had brought him invaluable advice in crossing fences from her husband Harvey, one of the world's all time greatest show jumpers. Richard knew that today he must 'hold the horse together', 'catch hold of its head' and let him pop over the fences. To allow him to 'stand off' a fence, a wonderful feeling on good ground, would see him on the floor.

Below: *Edmond falling at The Chair with (left to right) Blowing Wind, eventual winner Red Marauder, and Papillon*

The result, in Richard's words, was not always pretty, but his horsemanship was a supreme lesson in survival on horseback. The pair did brilliantly to keep together at the last Canal Turn, where a loose horse so nearly knocked them out, and again they survived a monumental blunder two fences later, four from home. This let Smarty go into the lead, giving backers of the Mark Pitman-trained horse renewed hope, but, as the pair came back across the Melling Road with only two more fences to negotiate, it was Red Marauder who was the stronger. He had defied gravity nearly a dozen times already and now he galloped on resolutely, popped the last fence and won by a distance, his ever-caring jockey dismounting immediately after the winning post.

Now spectators could look way back up the course and see two specks in the distance, with two more fences to jump and nearly a mile to run. Papillon and Blowing Wind could have won a prize

BELOW: *Tony McCoy (on Blowing Wind) chats to Ruby Walsh (on Papillon) during the race*

as a matching pair in a local hunter trial competition until the last fence was jumped, when it became a horse-race again. Blowing Wind was going better, so Tony McCoy turned in the saddle and, with a humorous wave, bade farewell to Papillon. Ruby Walsh, smiling beneath his mud-spattered face, waved back. In many ways, the gestures between the two jockeys summed up not only that particular race, but also the sport of steeplechasing in general. The Martell Grand National is a survivor, and the same can be said of the winning connections.

Barely two hours later, the bright red horsebox bearing Red Marauder was already emblazoned in Martell 2001 Grand National Winner logos as it headed home. In it was Red Marauder's devoted lass, Claire Metcalfe, herself one of the few women ever to have ridden over the Aintree fences.

Next morning, the nation's Press and television descended upon the 300-acre farm on top of the hills a few miles west of Durham. There, replenished frequently with Martell-provided

ABOVE: *Richard Guest with (left to right) Miss Martell, Norman Mason (owner/trainer), his wife Deborah and daughter Claire*

champagne, Norman Mason proudly relived the momentous 11 minutes of the race, the slowest since the mare Zoedone's in 1883, also run on heavy ground. The star of the show patiently posed for film crews and photographers until at last he was let into a walled paddock typical of the local Braes of Derwent Hunt country, along with companion Naphite. There, he had a buck and a skip and a squeal and then, after surveying the lofty scene, he nonchalantly rolled in the mud, oblivious to any dirt he might be inflicting on his gold-embossed winner's sheet placed over his outdoor rug.

After exactly half an hour, Richard Guest brought the horse back in. Richard, whose family is steeped in racing, had won the

Grand National and had been up all night celebrating, but nothing was going to stop him from doing what was right for the horse, not even national television. That is Richard all over. The horses are his life and always come first. Ironically, that is what had got him into trouble with the authorities three years earlier. Because he nurses horses, because he does not whip them, he had been found guilty, on an already beaten horse, of 'not trying'. Disillusioned, he handed in his licence. Fortunately for National Hunt racing in general and in particular Norman Mason, who praised Richard wholesomely as his 'miracle worker', the retirement was short-lived. Quite simply, Richard found it difficult to watch his charges from the grandstands, especially on the occasions he felt certain he could do better. He reapplied for his licence and the rest, as they say, is history. No one deserved the National win more than Richard – and Red Marauder.

In the Beginning: The First Steeplechase

It was in 1752, tradition has it, that two keen Irish fox-hunting gentlemen became responsible for the birth of steeplechasing. One can imagine a quiet moment with the waiting riders standing at covertside, the hounds drawing in vain for their quarry.

'Steeplechase Cracks' by John Frederick Herring Snr
(1795-1865)

ABOVE: *St John's Church, next to the old castle at Buttevant*

Chatter starts up, and before long it turns to the prowess of their respective hunters. 'I'll wager my horse is better than yours,' boasts Edmund Blake. 'I bet he could outrun yours from here to that steeple in the distance.'

'Prove it,' responds Cornelius O'Callaghan, 'and let a cask of wine ride on the outcome!'

It was soon arranged. The pair would start with their backs to St John's church, next to the old castle at Buttevant, and run down the steep slope to the banks of the River Awbeg, which joins the Blackwater a few miles away at Fermoy. From there, they would gallop by whatever line they chose to the distant steeple of St Mary's church at Doneraile, owned by the St Leger family, nearly five miles away.

The two gentlemen were friends of Sir Edmund O'Brien, 2nd baronet of Dromoland, whose mother was a first cousin of Queen Mary and Queen Anne. Sir Edmund fell in love so intensely with flat racing in Newmarket, England, that he renamed his village Newmarket-on-Fergus, and laid out a racetrack around Turret Hill, just north of Limerick in Co. Clare. It was there, in later years, that a manuscript was found containing details of that 'steeple to steeple chase', run from 'point-to-point' in Co. Cork.

Word of the wager between O'Callaghan and Blake soon spread, and people flocked to the spot on the appointed day.

After all, here was a novelty, for although there had been flat racing and betting since time immemorial, this race was to be different. The contestants would be jumping whatever obstacles happened to lie in their way.

Away down the slope they ran, jumping a tree log and splashing through the river, stirrup irons clanking as they knocked into each other in the deep water. On up the long hill they galloped, sweat beginning to fleck the hunters' necks as they reached the boreen, a sunken lane, at the top of the hill. They jumped off the bank into the lane, one stride and up the bank out of it.

Here, the area known as the Cahirmee opened up a little, and on they stretched across open farmland, in and out of more sunken lanes, the riders finding breath to curse and swear at each other if they got too close, or at their horses if they stumbled. They bypassed the boggy ground speckled with marsh marigolds, scrambled up and over more stone walls and somehow kept their seats, picking up their reins and urging their mounts ever faster, even bolder. They crashed through undergrowth and ducked under willows and waded through another loop in the river. Now they could see St Mary's church ahead of them and they spurred their horses on, each determined to win.

There is only one missing link to this story: the outcome. Perhaps that is just as well, for surely Edmund Blake and Cornelius O'Callaghan deserve to be remembered jointly for engendering a sport that has thrilled participants and spectators alike for the ensuing 250 years.

The scene of that race has changed little today. It took place in an area of Co. Cork, nestled in southern Ireland, which lies in the heart of the Duhallow Hunt country, where for 300 years fox-hunting has been an integral part of life. It will remain forever synonymous with steeplechasing: not only as the birthplace of the sport, but also as home to one Captain Martin

RIGHT: *St Mary's Church at Doneraile, owned by the St Leger family and nearly five miles away from Buttevant*

ABOVE: A brass plaque mounted on the wall of St Mary's Church commemorates the first recorded steeplechase run in 1752

Becher whose name was immortalised when he fell into a certain brook at Aintree. It was childhood home, too, to trainer Vincent O'Brien and jockey Jonjo O'Neill, and birthplace of triple Cheltenham Gold Cup winner Cottage Rake.

A few bungalows have sprung up beside the roads, but the original farmhouses still stand in splendid isolation at the end of tree-lined drives. The villages of Buttevant and Doneraile have tarmacked roads, of course, and electricity lines, and the motor car has largely replaced horse-drawn transport. Outside the stone walls of the St Leger's Doneraile Park, the grounds of which are open to the public, the sign for Doneraile announces that the village is twinned with Ramapo, New York. Opposite sits St Mary's church, and nailed to its gate is a plaque inscribed: 'In commemoration of the first recorded steeplechase run in

1752 from St. John's Church Buttevant to this St. Mary's Church Doneraile between Cornelius O'Callaghan and Edmund Blake over a distance of 4½ miles erected by D.C.D.C. June 1996.'

From here, the road slopes downhill to the village centre and the River Awbeg. More shops and houses stretch away uphill on the far side. It is a scene more than a little familiar to Jonjo O'Neill, one of steeplechasing's greats, who, as a boy, had to cycle to school in Doneraile from his home at Castletownroche seven miles away. Buttevant, with its wide main road, is slightly larger, but essentially neither village has altered much over the years.

When Cheltenham Racecourse staged the Buttevant Hunters' Steeplechase on St Patrick's Day, 17 March 1995, its commercial manager, Peter McNiele, wrote to the Buttevant town hall inviting its mayor (if it had one) to present the trophy. A telephone call confirmed that the mayor would be attending. The steeplechase was held as part of a fourth day following the Festival, because the remaining meetings that year could not take place due to drainage work being carried out. A fortnight before the Cheltenham Festival, an anonymous phone call reported that the mayor who intended to come was an imposter. Peter McNiele takes up the story: 'We had visions of Buttevant civil servants fighting it out on the presentation podium. In the event, a charming little Irishman who appeared presented his trophy most courteously and no shenanigans took place! But I don't believe he is listed in *Who's Who* . . .' There is, in fact, no mayor of Buttevant.

The tract of land between Buttevant and Doneraile is farmed in the traditional way, and much of it has been in the hands of the same families for fifty years or more: the O'Neills, Sheahans, Caseys, Barrys, Nevilles and Walshes. Inevitably, there is some wire, and one or two neat hedges, but there are still patches of marsh and woodland, and crumbling stone walls, and the sunken lanes or boreens, so that when a 'rerun' was staged in 1954, the country would not have been so very different from two centuries before. It is not as hairy as some parts of Ireland, which have massive banks, often topped by thorns, and yawning ditches, but it takes some crossing by a brave horse and rider nevertheless. One rider in 1954, Jerome Casey, a well-known show rider, paid no heed to Willie O'Brien's shouted warning of a steep drop ahead coming out of Cahirmee – perhaps believing it to be a piece of jockeyship designed to slow down a rival – and plunged headlong into the track beneath the bank, breaking his leg.

Willie O'Brien lives at Spitalfields just outside Buttevant, where today, at the age of seventy-eight, he runs a thriving bed and breakfast with his daughter. In the 1954 race, he finished second on Glenville to the great P.P. Hogan riding Bay Park. Pat Hogan was the leading amateur rider of his day and Field Master to the Scarteen hounds. He was universally acknowledged as a brilliant horseman, and Vincent O'Brien considered him the best judge of a horse in the country.

There were two main differences between the race in 1954 and the original race: first, that it was run the other way round from Doneraile to Buttevant, because that way spectators had a better view of the finish; and second, there were fifty-three riders instead of two. The hunting connection was maintained with a prize for the best hunt team of three, won by the Killeagh, whose Billy and Brian McLernan finished third and fourth overall in the race. The local Duhallow Hunt fielded four teams and the other teams represented the Kildare (which included film director John Huston and the USA's veteran amateur rider Tim Durant, who made several forays on the Grand National in the 1960s); the Avondhu; the Scarteen (Black and Tans), who fielded the winner; the Tipperary; and the United Hunts. Following tradition, the winner received a hogshead of wine.

The world's biggest purse for a steeplechase today is in Japan. The winner of the 2001 Grand National was due to receive £290,000 from a total fund of £500,000 going down to sixth place (£7,500). The Corinthian spirit survives, however, and steeplechasing has never fallen to the big business or 'mega bucks' of the flat racing scene.

Almost all of the male horses running in National Hunt races are geldings; therefore, they cannot be used for breeding at the end of their careers. Usually, barring accidents, this means they race for far longer than the majority of their flat brethren, so they often become much-loved household names. The mares that win steeplechases can, and often do, become successful brood mares.

There is a tendency today to refer to 'jump' racing, but the words National Hunt, steeple (to steeple) chasing and point-to-point all stem from the sport's foundation in hunting. Hunting still plays its part, both as a nursery school for future steeplechasers and as a retirement home for old or failed ones.

Early Portraits: Artists' Impressions

At about the time that photography was in its crude infancy, and well before it could be used out of doors, steeplechasing was evolving from the straight matches between two hunters to organised races over a prepared course. The most reliable pictorial records, therefore, lie in the sporting art of the time, especially in the years leading up to the first Grand National in 1839.

'The Vale of Aylesbury Steeplechase' by F.C. Turner (1795–1846). Vivian is leading the field at Fleet Maiston Brook

It was the custom of the nobility and gentry in the eighteenth century to commission paintings for their grand new mansions: usually they were of their hunters or flat race horses, but increasingly they were of their steeplechasers too.

A new business grew up in making prints of the paintings, usually coloured etchings and aquatints, enabling them to be purchased by a wider market. Coloured etchings originated in Switzerland: Johann Ludwig Aberli (1723–86) etched outlines of landscapes and paintings of costumes, and employed and trained assistants to copy enough to satisfy the tourist trade. Among the best known early sporting artists were Francis Barlow (1626–1702); Peter Tillemans (1684–1734); John Wootton (c. 1683–1764); and George Stubbs (1724–1806). Nineteenth-century artists included John Frederick Herring Snr, who was Dutch by birth, T.H. Bird, W.B. Wollen, and J. H. Thornely. Among the first to colour sporting prints were James Seymour, Thomas Spencer, Sartorius and Henry Roberts. Those who made a name for themselves for producing prints and engravings included J. Harris, E. Duncan, Charles Hunt and his relative, George Hunt, and R.G. Reeve.

It was George Stubbs, the great British animal artist, who was one of the first to include serious sporting subjects. A little later, the prolific Henry Alken, who was born of Danish parents in 1785 and died penniless in 1851, painted the series of the 'Midnight Steeplechase', said to have been run in 1803 but more likely to have been fictitious. Alken produced an endless stream of paintings, drawings, prints and book illustrations. He also hunted, which doubtless helped to produce the authenticity in his work. But he made one surprising mistake in his series of the 'Midnight Steeplechase': one picture showed a rider jumping a broken gate, but the shadow depicted an unbroken gate, and there was no shadow at all of the horse and rider. This set of four was originally published by Ackermann, but a second issue by Ben Brooks rectified the shadow mistakes. However, some of these copies have had the original shadowing mistakes re-inked, in an attempt to deceive buyers looking for a first issue.

The race is supposed to have taken place near Nacton, Essex, between young officers stationed at Ipswich barracks, for a bet on the merits of their horses. They are shown wearing nightshirts over their uniforms and nightcaps. In America, inspired by the story, a number of moonlight steeplechases were organised, the first in 1897 over a $1\frac{3}{4}$-mile course of seven whitewashed board fences. The moonlight was sporadic that night, but it produced a grand duel between the winner, a horse called Tom Clark, from a mare called Nancy Lee. Further races were run in 1910 and 1930, and probably several more, shrouded in secrecy.

The first made-up course was laid out at Bedford in 1810, with eight fences of 4ft 6in (the same height as today) on the circuit. The race was to be run in heats, and the horses had to be certified as having been 'in at the death' of three foxes in Leicestershire. Point-to-pointers today have to be certified hunters, but without that added stipulation. Matches between hunters over a line of unknown country remained the primary competition for a few more decades, but the Bedford course was a landmark in the evolution of steeplechasing.

Two of England's first steeplechasing entrepreneurs were Thomas Coleman and William Lynn. Between them, they can take much of the credit for making the sport more popular. Until their involvement, fox-hunting was the number one priority of the riding gentry, especially the cavalry officers returning from the Napoleonic Wars which culminated in the Battle of Waterloo in 1815.

In 1830, Thomas Coleman organised the St Alban's Steeplechase, the forerunner in prestige to the Grand National, which was founded in 1839 by William Lynn (see pp. 36–47). The St Alban's Chase was run over four miles from Hartlington Church to the obelisk in Wrest Park, and was won by Lord Ranelagh's grey, Wonder, ridden by Captain MacDowell, a guards officer.

'Tommy' Coleman was an early steeplechasing aficionado with an eye for the main chance. He bought the Chequers Hotel

'The Midnight Steeplechase'; one of a series painted by Henry Alken

PAGES 30–31: *'A Steeplechase' by John Frederick Herring Jnr*

(1815–1907)

ABOVE: *'The Vale of Aylesbury Steeplechase' by F.C. Turner (1795–1846). Vivian comes in past the winning post, followed by Grimaldi, and The Pony*

in the town, renamed it the Turf Hotel and installed the luxuries of running water and baths. With so many visitors on race days, buckets were filled with beer so that mugs could be dipped in for speed of service.

One of the sport's first great duels was illustrated by Henry Alken in six plates he produced in 1827 entitled simply 'Steeplechases'. It was a match that was spoken of with admiration and awe for many years, as the matches between Golden Miller and Thomond II, Arkle and Mill House, and Monksfield and Sea Pigeon would be in a later century. Clinker and Radical were the two horses, the year was 1826, and the line chosen was

some four miles across country between Barkby Holt and Billesdon Coplow in prime Leicestershire hunting country.

Captain Ross had such confidence in Mr Francis Holyoake's Clinker that he backed himself to ride him against any horse Lord Kennedy cared to choose. This was some dare, and Lord Kennedy scoured the country to find the most suitable challenger. The answer was Thomas Assheton-Smith's Radical, with Captain Douglas to ride.

There was plenty of pre-race 'needle' between the protagonists, and spectators flocked to watch from miles around. It had been agreed in advance that it should be 'a race to the death'. So the scene was set, and thousands of pounds were staked on the outcome; Lord Kennedy himself wagered £2,000. In a pre-race trial, in which Clinker was ridden by leading professional Dick Christian, he clocked up a time over the course of 11 minutes 15 seconds. Captain Douglas, on board Radical, was acknowledged as a superior rider to hounds, but Captain Ross, better known as a marksman, had the advantage of knowing the Leicestershire countryside well.

The race proved an anticlimax. The first obstacle in their way was a five-barred gate, and as they approached it, Ross had Clinker about half a length up on Radical. But the quick-witted Ross could see that Radical looked like refusing, so he held Clinker back and then, as Radical duly swung across the front of the gate, he pushed Clinker into his opponent's side, knocking Douglas over his horse's head. Ross quickly turned and popped Clinker over the gate. Although Captain Douglas remounted Radical and set off in hot pursuit, Captain Ross and Clinker had gone beyond recall.

Thomas Assheton-Smith, Radical's owner, and Squire George Osbaldeston were the country's two leading huntsmen. Assheton-Smith hunted the Quorn hounds in Leicestershire and then, for thirty-two seasons, the Tedworth in Wiltshire and Hampshire, while the Squire took over the Quorn hounds, before 'retiring' to the Pytchley. But whereas the Squire fully supported the newfangled sport of steeplechasing, Assheton-Smith emphatically did not, believing it to be unfair and too rough on the horses, taking more out of them than a whole day's hunting. It is fitting that more than two centuries later it was a horse called Osbaldeston that put jockey John Francome on the map. What is more, when Assheton-Smith sold Radical, reputedly for 500 guineas, he is said to have remarked, 'Whoever rides him must be as strong as an elephant, as bold as a lion and as quiet as a mouse'. The Dikler, winner of the 1973 Cheltenham Gold Cup, springs to mind as another for whom this would be an apt description.

For some time no one would oppose Clinker until, in 1830, Squire Osbaldeston backed his Clasher for £1,000 to beat him. As usual, the race came about as a result of some bragging. Captain Becher and Captain Ross were extolling the virtues of Clinker after dinner, when Squire Osbaldeston said he would take him on with Clasher, a dark bay he had bought from a farmer. Captain Becher laughed, thinking the Squire meant it as

a joke. When he saw Osbaldeston was serious, the match was made, to be run at level weights over the five miles of country from Great Dalby Windmill to a spot near Tilton on the Hill. Captain Ross stipulated that Dick Christian would ride Clinker, but the Squire elected to ride his own horse, even though he had been badly hurt in the hunting field. Clasher was said to be an 'extraordinary fencer and a capital water jumper'.

In Henry Alken's picture of the race, he paints the rolling Leicestershire landscape at the time of the match, with many mounted spectators and quite a few children but no women to be seen. He shows that the Squire wore green, and Dick Christian blue. Dick Christian, based at Melton Mowbray, was one of the era's leading professional horse trainers, riding masters and jockeys; he had also been a head groom and a whipper-in. He often appears in sporting prints, and seems to have been one of the few 'plebs' to have been accepted socially by the sporting aristocracy.

Again before the race there was plenty of goading between the respective parties. Squire Osbaldeston was mindful of the hunting fall which had partly crippled him; it was not the fall that had hurt him, but a rider who followed him too closely, was brought down and landed on top of him. Before the race, he told Dick, 'I know what your orders are, but I do ask one thing: that you don't jump on me if I fall.'

Dick replied, 'I'll give you my word, Squire, I won't.'

It proved a cracking race, with the pair running neck and neck until Dick tried a new ploy. He called out, 'Squire, you're beat for £100', and with that he swung off in a different direction, for in his pre-race reconnaissance he had discovered a ford in Twyford Brook. His cunning, however, did not pay off, as the Squire and Clasher leapt the brook 'with a yard to spare'. Nevertheless, it was a close race, for Clasher was only just ahead when their paths met up again, but Clinker fell at the last. The Squire, renowned huntsman that he was, won all six steeplechase matches that he took part in.

An undoubted star of the time was a striking grey horse called

The World's Greatest Steeplechase: The Grand National

The Grand National drew the crowds – and the publicity – right from its very first running, when it was won by the appropriately named Lottery.

The 1939 Grand National: the eventual winner, Lottery, is in the centre of the picture; his jockey wears a blue jacket. Engraving by J. Harris.

LONDON, PUBLISHED MAY 1ST 1839, BY THOS MCLEAN, 26, HAYMARKET.

Mr Elmore's
Lottery.

Mr Wm Haddy's
Cannon Ball.

Mr J H Leeche's
Charity.

Sir E Mostyns
Seventy Four.

Lord McDonald's
The Nun.

ENGRAVED BY J. HARRIS

GREAT NATIONAL STEEPLE-CHASE, 1839.

The pre-publicity hype surrounding hotelier William Lynn's initiative in 1839 was so successful that innkeepers in the area were cramming in four people per bed the night before the race. The streets thronged with spectators (an estimated 50,000) making their way to the course at Aintree on foot, by omnibus or horse-drawn cab; vendors sold their wares along the way, and pickpockets had a field day. Entrance to the stands was 7/- (35p). Among the syndicate

ABOVE: *A drawing of Captain Martin Becher who rode Conrad in the first Grand National in 1839. An incident during that race led to the name Becher's Brook being given to one of the fences*

helping Lynn stage the race was one Edward William Topham, a name which became synonymous with the running of the race.

Even in those early days, there existed a tradition of rivalry between the English and the Irish, and among the fifty-five entries for the four-mile Grand Liverpool Steeplechase were several from across the Irish Sea competing for the £1,200 purse.

The prize fund for 2001 was £500,000, with entrance prices ranging from £10 for the Steeplechase Enclosure, situated well away from the stands on the far side of the Melling Road at the Canal Turn and on the Embankment, to £25 for the Tattersalls Enclosure and £65 for the other stands, such as County, Queen Mother and Aldaniti.

On Tuesday, 26 February 1839, seventeen runners faced the starter, including most of the best known horses of the day, such as Rust and Daxon from Ireland. Lottery, ridden by Jem Mason, was the favourite, and other fancied runners included a mare, The Nun, and Charity. The Nun was found to be 'too fat' and so was taken off for a 'severe' gallop two hours before the race, delaying its start. The conditions allowed for 'no rider to open a gate or ride through a gateway, or more than 100 yards along any road footpath, or driftway'. So long as marker flags were passed on the correct side, riders could choose almost any course, much as they had in the first steeplechases in the 1750s.

The original Aintree fences were much smaller than today, mostly sprigs of gorse atop two-foot banks with a ditch either on the take-off or landing side. There were also one or two posts and rails, but there was a notable exception: a stone wall nearly five feet high in front of the grandstand (flat racing had been in existence at Aintree for ten years), close to where the water jump is sited now. The last two fences were sheep hurdles. In addition, there were two brooks which had been dammed, making them about eight feet wide. The first, to be immortalised by Captain Becher in the first running of the race, had a strong timber fence of about 3ft 6in set a yard in front of it and was approached over deep plough. The second, which became known as Valentine's Brook after the horse which finished third in 1840, had a two-foot earth mound in front of the brook, acting as a guard-rail, and on the far side was a three-foot timber fence with a considerable drop on landing. Stretches of plough remained until 1950 – there having been a potato patch to cross that year – and for nearly the first half century of the race there used to be more plough than turf.

With a cheer from the crowds, the runners for the inaugural

running, in ground described as 'deep', were off, led by Daxon and Captain Becher's mount, Conrad, 'taking each other on' at a cracking pace until they approached Brook No 1. Here, memorably, Captain Becher fell, took refuge in the brook, and is purported to have said the water tasted foul without either whiskey or brandy in it. Naturally, the brook has borne his name ever since. Captain Becher remounted, but fell again, and this time the wise Conrad ran off loose. Before long, Daxon, too, had fallen and his Irish compatriot, Rust, had been 'kidnapped' up a lane by those whose money was on another horse, and was not freed until all hope of victory had gone. To the surprise of many, Charity, trained in the Cotswolds, fell at the wall, which Lottery

BELOW: *Lottery, the celebrated Grand National winner, drawn by John Frederick Herring Snr*

jumped superbly before setting out on the second circuit. The Nun faded; Dictator fell and was remounted, only to fall dead at the very next fence, which caused the sort of outcry that has been a part of the race ever since; Paulina began to fade. As Lottery sailed into the lead, it was clear he was going the best by far. In fact, he is said to have cleared the final hurdle with a leap that measured thirty-three feet and won 'in a canter'. Only Seventy-Four, ridden by 'Black Tom' Olliver, got anywhere near him. Paulina finished a poor third, True Blue fourth, The Nun fifth, Railroad sixth and Pioneer seventh and last. Rust was recorded as pulled up, while Dictator, Conrad, Cramp, Rambler, Daxon, Barkston, Cannon Ball, Jack and Charity all fell. Lottery earned such a reputation that in some future races conditions expressly forbade him from running or else weighted him down with an impossible burden.

For its first 100 years, the Grand National was the pinnacle which every owner, trainer and jockey aspired to scale. But once the Gold Cup, founded in 1924, became well established in the 1930s, that race became the Blue Riband, mainly because horses were competing on a level playing field instead of being handicapped.

The Grand National has, however, always captured the imagination of a world-wide audience, and remains the most famous race globally, with some 600 million viewers, including, for the first time in 2001, live coverage in China.

BELOW: *The Grand National in 1912: Jerry M is led in*

In 1841, for the third running of the race, the organisers bowed to pressure, following mishaps, and removed the wall, replacing it with an artificial brook ten feet wide and three feet deep, with a thick thorn fence on the take-off side. The water jump today measures 9ft 6in wide, six inches deep and the fence in front of it is 2ft 9in high.

In 1843, the name of the race changed to the Liverpool and National Steeplechase, and it became a handicap race for the first time. Previously, the weights had been weight for age, or a level twelve stone, as the Cheltenham Gold Cup is today (bar a five pound allowance for mares). In 1843, the new handicap specified a top weight of 12st 8lb, but a winner after the date of

declaration was penalised five pounds. The favourite, Peter Simple, carried 13st 1lb, and came home eighth of nine finishers, just behind Lottery on 12st 6lb. The wall was back in for this race only, but stood at four feet with a layer of turf on top, similar to the wall at Auteuil today. The going that year was described as 'hard but good', and Tom Olliver rode the winner, Vanguard. In 1847, the race first took on the name of the Grand National Handicap Steeplechase and was won by Matthew. A year later, Mr Topham took over the lease of Aintree and became Clerk of the Course. By 1856, Messrs Topham became responsible for the management of the race.

In 1863, the course was lengthened by about a quarter of a mile, but for the most part the fences were still very low. Becher's and Valentine's, however, were stiffened by the addition of a post and rail put up in front of each. The only other fences considered at all difficult were the open ditch and the water. The race that year was won by Emblem, one of five winning rides in the race for George Stevens between 1856 and 1870. This was an era when the Grand National was at a low ebb, and had even fallen into disrepute, along with steeplechasing in general, until it was picked up and regenerated by the National Hunt Committee, formed in 1866, which had its own official calendar and code of rules. This body soon had the sport – and the great race – thriving again, but nothing should detract from the part George Stevens played in its history.

So small that he looked as if a puff of wind would blow him over, he could easily have done the weight to ride on the Flat. Instead he left his home on Cleeve Hill, overlooking Cheltenham racecourse, to become a steeplechase jockey. His mentor was Tom Olliver, second in the inaugural running of the Grand National, placed several other times and winner thrice, in 1842 on Gaylad, in the following year on Vanguard and in 1853 on Peter Simple.

George Stevens first masterminded the concept 'hunt round on the first circuit'. Even on a horse with suspect stamina, he could successfully come at the end of a race with winning speed, because the horse had been in 'third gear' in the rear for most of it. He was the original master of the waiting race, of judging pace, of timing a run to perfection. After his first win in the National, on Free Trader in 1856, a bonfire was lit on Cleeve Hill to commemorate his achievement, a mark of honour that was to be repeated in 1863 (Emblem), 1864 (Emblematic), and twice more, in 1869 and 1870, when he was victorious on The Colonel.

Emblem and Emblematic were lightly boned, flat race-bred full sisters on whom George Stevens was seen at his stamina-conserving best, but The Colonel was a much more robust-looking fellow with good bone and size. Yet again, George Stevens let those up front run themselves out of it or fall while he 'hunted' quietly along at the back, going the shortest way and steering clear of trouble. For his final, record-breaking fifth National win, again on The Colonel, he found himself taken on at his own game, with George Holman shadowing him the whole way on a horse called The Doctor. In consequence, they produced a thrilling finish, with Stevens' superior strength and experience in the saddle just prevailing. Sadly, shortly after his retirement only three months after his second win on The Colonel, George Stevens was thrown from his cob close to his home on Cleeve Hill, and killed.

George Stevens rode more than 100 winners in his career, including those five Grand Nationals. Now, more than 150 years on, it is almost a certainty that one or more jockeys will ride that number in a year – or, in the cases of Peter Scudamore and Tony McCoy, an incredible 221 (1988–9) and 253 (1997–8) respectively.

The year 1883 saw the smallest field in the history of the Grand National when, on ground described as 'very heavy', just ten runners went to post. The race was won by a mare called Zoedone, ridden by her owner, Count Charles Kinsky. The count was an Austrian who raced in a truly amateur spirit. He wanted to buy the mare for the race, but could not afford her. Then he won the Cesarewitch, worth £1,000, enabling him to buy Zoedone for £800 with a £200 contingency should she win the National. The six-year-old chestnut mare was slow, but she could jump and possessed abundant stamina. The count was advised to 'hunt round' on the first circuit – an instruction that is still often given. He did just that, then looked around to sum up his rivals, kicked on and outstayed and outjumped the opposition, drawing clear in the home straight.

The race readers of 1884, one year before the course was railed in, had an impossible task, as the mist was so thick that they could see very little of the race. It was won by Voluptuary, bred by Queen Victoria for the Derby without success. He was a hurdle winner, but had never jumped a steeplechase fence in

BELOW: *Manifesto, winner of the Grand National in 1897 and 1899, shown here with jockey George Williamson*

public before the National, though he was said to jump all obstacles when out hunting.

The year 1893, when the ground was described as 'very hard and dry' and the weather as 'sunny and hot', saw the magnificent Cloister gallop to the widest winning margin (until 2001) of forty lengths, carrying 12st 7lb. By this time, the fences were big and uniformly much as they are today, though in 1961 the take-off sides were sloped out and in 1989 most of the ditch on the landing side of Becher's was filled in.

When The Soarer won the 1896 running, the purse had increased to £2,500. The 1898 running was on 'very heavy and bad' ground in a 'blinding snowstorm'. The horse to gallop through it first was Drogheda.

ABOVE: *Trainer Robert Gore with Covertcoat, winner of the Grand National in 1913*

Cloister was one of the National 'greats'. Another, a few years later, was Manifesto, who, on the written evidence, has become one of my own favourites. He ran in the race no less than eight times, from the ages of seven to sixteen years, between 1895 and 1904, won it twice, was third three times and as a sixteen-year-old had to carry 12st 1lb.

In 1900, he was third carrying 12st 13lb, giving up to forty-eight pounds to some horses. Arkle once had to give forty-nine pounds, but not in the National. The race was won by the Prince of Wales' Ambush II, but the brave Manifesto, giving twenty-four pounds to the royal runner, drew level at the second last. It was only 100 yards from the line, at the end of that long, gruelling run-in, that Manifesto was defeated. Barsac, carrying just 9st 12lb – that is, 3st 1lb less than Manifesto – stole second place on the line.

Snow returned in 1901, when the ground was 'very deep, and the course white with snow'; again, the race was run in a 'blinding snowstorm'. This is the race for which owner Bernard Bletsoe enterprisingly smeared butter on the feet of his home-bred and -trained Grudon to prevent the snow from balling up, and it probably helped him to victory. Moifaa, a horse who survived a shipwreck on his way over from New Zealand, won in 1904, the year of Manifesto's last appearance.

By 1912, the race distance was established at 4 miles 856 yards, as it is today. For the first time, the breeder of the winner received 100 sovereigns, though today there is no specific monetary prize for the breeder, from the race purse. The race was worth £3,500, including a trophy valued at £125; the lowest weight was set at ten stone, as it is today. The winner that year

was Jerry M, carrying top weight of 12st 7lb, trained at Findon by Robert Gore and ridden by Lester Piggott's grandfather, Ernie, who rode three Grand National winners. The owner, Sir Charles Assheton-Smith, won again the following year with Covertcoat, and had also owned Cloister.

From 1916 to 1918 the race was run at Gatwick, on ground now covered by the runways of London's second international airport. The conditions were the same as when it had been run at Aintree, except that the first race was worth only £500, and was called the Race Course Association Steeplechase; in 1917 it was christened the War National. The winner in 1918 was Poethlyn. He proved his rightful place in the roll of honour by winning again in 1919 when the race was back at Aintree; on both occasions he was ridden by Ernie Piggott.

ABOVE: *Battleship, the first American-bred horse to win the Grand National, leading at Becher's Brook*

The 1921 winner, Shaun Spadah, was the only one of thirty-five runners not to fall, although three others remounted to finish. In 1924, skull caps became compulsory, following the death on Boxing Day of Captain Tuppy Bennet, who had won the previous year's National on Sergeant Murphy, the first American-owned horse to win. This period between the wars saw a keen American interest, culminating in tiny Battleship's victory of 1938.

The race had been broadcast on radio since 1927, and was reaching a wider audience. The following year, 1928, was a broadcaster's nightmare, when Easter Hero, the class horse in the race, galloped into a clear lead but at the Canal Turn took off too soon and got straddled. In a scene that was to be almost carbon-copied in 2001, a handful of horses got through but then the rest were baulked, refused, unseated their riders, putting out twenty runners in one blow. After another circuit had been run on the very heavy ground, only three horses remained and one of these, Great Span, who looked the likely winner, had his saddle slip, causing his luckless jockey to be tipped off – a foretaste of Carl Llewellyn losing his reins on Beau in 2001 in

similar conditions. Billy Barton fell at the last with the race at his mercy, leaving the only other horse still standing, Tipperary Tim, to win at 100–1.

The next year, 1929, saw an all-time record number of sixty-six runners (there is now a safety limit of forty), and only ten finished, led home by another 100–1 shot, Gregalach. There was also a record crowd, said to be some 300,000.

After two consecutive 100–1 winners, the 1930 result proved more predictable, with the second favourite, Shaun Goilin, beating the not unfancied mare, Melleray's Belle, with the second favourite, Sir Lindsay, coming in third. These three rose in the air almost together over the last fence. All three jockeys lost stirrup irons here. In a thrilling finish, Shaun Goilin won by a head.

The favourite, Grakle, had fallen, but his turn came the next year in 1931, when Easter Hero was back in the race and favourite, having won two Cheltenham Gold Cups. The sun was shining and the ground was perfect. No less than thirty of the forty-three runners were still there at the end of the first circuit, though Easter Hero was among the fallers on the second. The finish saw a memorable duel between Grakle and Gregalach, who had at one time been stable companions. Grakle wore a type of cross noseband which has born his name ever since.

The 1930s saw some class horses producing fast times and an added injection was given to the prestige of the race by the amount of international interest. War was to intervene, although the race was held in both 1939 before hostilities were declared and in 1940 when there was still the 'phoney' war. Timmy Hyde and Workman won the 1939 race for Ireland; in 1940 it was England's turn with Bogskar, who beat the Scottish horse, MacMoffat.

In the six years that followed with no race possible, it was often felt that Tom Dreaper's Prince Regent lost his chance. By

LEFT: *Battleship, aboard the liner* Manhattan *en route back to the USA, being fed by his seventeen-year-old jockey Bruce Hobbs*

1946, Prince Regent was eleven years old, but he was allocated 12st 5lb. It was too much. He was still clear at the last fence under Timmy Hyde, but the combination of weight and that long run-in of 494 yards took its toll. He was overtaken by Lovely Cottage ridden by Captain Bobby Petre and then by Jack Finlay.

The 1950s began desperately for the race's reputation. In 1951, the starter pressed the button when many were still checking girths, adjusting caps or stirrups – anything but coming forward into line, shortening reins, adrenaline pumping. As a result, they set off in hot pursuit of those who had got away on cue, went too fast, and twelve either fell or were brought down at the first fence. From Becher's second time round, only two runners remained in the race, victory going to Nickel Coin. It was the year that Mrs Mirabel Topham, an actress, forward

BELOW: *The field taking the first jump at the Grand National in 1928. It was won by Tipperary Tim, the only competitor not to fall out of a field of forty-two starters*

thinker and doughty character, began her hands-on involvement as race manager.

There was blundering of a different type in 1952. Mrs Topham and her Aintree executive fell out with the British Broadcasting Corporation over the matter of copyright. The deadlock could not be resolved and Mrs Topham was convinced the management could do the broadcast. The resultant shambles from rank amateurs only underlined the polish and professionalism that the BBC had shown since first broadcasting the race in 1927. That was no consolation to the thousands of radio listeners. One writer described the attempt at commentary as 'comic crosstalk which told listeners precious little about the race'.

Radio broadcasts had helped the Grand National, but when the BBC first televised the race in 1960 it affected the attendance, as potential spectators preferred to view the race from the comfort of their armchairs and to listen to the dulcet tones of Peter O'Sullevan. It is doubtful whether his prowess as a racing commentator will ever be surpassed. If he had backed a horse or owned a runner, he never let it show. When there was a huge

field to decipher, he remained cerebrally nimble. Even when his own Attivo was winning the Triumph Hurdle at Cheltenham, he stayed cool, calm, collected – and accurate. His last broadcast was of Suny Bay's Hennessy in 1996, when he was seventy-eight years old; it was as polished as ever. In the race, Graham Bradley lifted the grey horse off the floor after a monumental mistake. The win put him up in the weights, and Suny Bay subsequently finished runner-up in the next two Grand Nationals, to Lord Gyllene in 1997 and Earth Summit in 1998. Suny Bay was retired in January 2001.

Peter O'Sullevan, bestowed with a knighthood in 1997 shortly before he retired, missed the Martell Grand National in April 2001 for the first time in more than fifty years because of an operation. 'I broke down in my off fore, the artery packed up,' he joked, 'then the near fore went and I had to have a second operation a week after the National.' But the ever youthful octogenarian not only made it to Sandown at the end of that month, but could also be seen striding up the track when he went to assist a fallen horse. In retirement he finds himself busier than ever, and is very involved in animal welfare charities.

Another familiar face missing from Aintree was Bob Champion, who suffered a heart attack. It was the first time in some thirty years that 1981's winning rider was absent. Very much there on duty, however, was Peter Bromley who was to radio commentary what Peter O'Sullevan was to television. It was his forty-second and final radio commentary on the Grand National, and afterwards he was presented with a memento by Aintree chairman Lord Daresbury.

The mid-1960s to 1970s became the decade of 'the last Grand National' at Aintree, when various property development deals were flying about. In 1975, Ladbrokes, the bookmakers, signed an eight-year deal with new owner Bill Davies to manage the race, but he was then reluctant to renew the contract, wishing, instead, to sell the site for development. Again the Grand National's destiny hung in the balance. Finally, with the help of a public subscription, the Jockey Club was able to buy Aintree

ABOVE: *Sir Peter O' Sullevan*

and save the great race for posterity.

In 1975, Mr Davies' last year, he tripled the admission price and saw attendance fall to an all-time low of around 10,000, as many people elected to sit back and watch Red Rum on the box. (In 2001, the world-wide TV viewing audience was an estimated 600 million.) Since the late 1970s, with the supportive sponsorship of Seagram and its subsidiary, Martell, coupled with imaginative and efficient organisation, the whole event has blossomed into a racing festival worthy of the world's greatest horse race.

A Little Diversion: Hurdling

The future King George IV, when Prince of Wales acting as Prince Regent, may well have been responsible for the first hurdle race and, as with steeplechasing, its origins lay in hunting or, in this instance, as a diversion during a poor day's hunting.

Tim Moloney takes Sir Ken over the last flight to go on and win the Champion Hurdle Challenge Cup, Cheltenham, 1953. It was Sir Ken's 16th successive win over hurdles and the second victory in this event

horse he once was, and was deservedly retired to the hunting field.

During this period, riding continued to evolve, and one or two riders made their name as hurdle race jockeys, notably Johnny Haine (Salmon Spray) and Jimmy Uttley (Persian War). Dick Francis noted in his 1957 autobiography, *The Sport of Queens*, that Continental riders consistently adopted a much more forward seat over their fences and hurdles. The forward, or 'monkey on a stick' style, had been used on the Flat since the turn of the twentieth century, when American rider Tod Sloan brought it to these shores. It was a style that balanced a horse better and offered less wind resistance, enabling it to use its speed and action to better effect. But the natural self-preservation requirement of jockeys riding jumpers meant that they retained a more upright style for considerable time to come.

The reason why the French jockeys began to crouch more when hurdling, Dick Francis said, was that their obstacles were much softer; therefore, when a horse hit one, it was rarely unbalanced. Built of birch, about 3ft 8in high, French hurdles are softer than our steeplechase fences, but the birch is upright. On both sides of the hurdle there is a two-foot ditch with a white painted guard-rail so that they can be, and are, jumped from either direction. Because they are so different, it is not surprising that very few English-trained horses have excelled over them, an exception being the mare Dawn Run, who memorably won the French Champion Hurdle in 1984, after winning the English equivalent.

In 1954, as an experiment, French hurdles were introduced in Britain. At first, their virtues were extolled, as there were few injuries to the horses, either from falling or from rapping the hurdles. But when those same horses switched to chasing, many fell because they were unaccustomed to such stiffness, and the experiment was abandoned. Today the question of hurdle design is being seriously addressed again, in particular by trainer Ferdy Murphy in Yorkshire. Unhappy with traditional hurdles,

even calling them 'barbaric', he said horses could get hurt when rapped, and suggested the introduction of French-style hurdles should be considered once more.

One of the most courageous battlers ever was Monksfield, winner of the Champion Hurdle in 1978 and 1979. He, too, was bought cheaply, but was a robust character and soon showed his mettle. He was second in the 1977 Champion Hurdle to Night Nurse, winning his second crown under Paddy Broderick; Night Nurse made a successful transition to chasing and finished second in the 1981 Cheltenham Gold Cup.

The Champion Hurdle of 1978 was vintage: Night Nurse and Monksfield went hammer and tongs, head for head, stride for stride. Night Nurse gave way, but poised to swoop was Sea Pigeon. 'Monkey' simply refused to give in and scored by two lengths. The following year was even closer and the chief protagonists were the same. This time, as Monksfield and Sea Pigeon headed flat out for the last fight together, it was Monksfield who came under pressure. Sea Pigeon went ahead – in fact, Jonjo O'Neill blames himself for coming too soon. Monksfield, finding himself headed, responded with the sort of courage that marks the truly great from the good. He simply refused to be beaten, and it was to the benefit of future generations that, as an entire horse, he was later able to stand at stud.

Of all the many top-class horses Jonjo O'Neill rode, he rates Sea Pigeon the best 'because he was so fast'. Sea Pigeon was a nearly black son of outstanding Derby and Arc winner Sea Bird II. Sea Pigeon was highly strung and had a mind of his own; he had to be 'covered up' in a race, only hitting the front just before the winning post, when he could unleash his speed. This, as we saw against Monksfield, was not always possible, but few horses come as difficult to beat as 'Monkey'. Sea Pigeon won just over half of his hurdle races during his career. These included one Welsh and two Scottish Champion Hurdles as well as two crowns at Cheltenham.

His turns for the Champion Hurdle came in 1980 for Jonjo O'Neill and the following year for Johnny Francome. Jonjo declared that his win came in spite of the fact that Sea Pigeon, having been held up in his work at home, 'blew up' a mile from the finish. The classy horse let out the 'most disturbing gasps and pants'. Jonjo bided his time, knowing Sea Pigeon was not a horse to be hustled or told what to do. Then, having gained his second wind, Sea Pigeon galloped into the last flight a length down on his old adversary, Monksfield. Jonjo said, 'Sea Pigeon propelled us over and away in one single act of graceful power that swept us shoulder to shoulder with Monksfield and Dessie Hughes.' Even then, he feared he had come too soon again, but this time Sea Pigeon, class Derby-bred horse that he was, 'produced a flash of overdrive', giving an experience of speed under the saddle that Jonjo had never before felt in a jumper. He put seven lengths between himself and the gallant Monksfield.

BELOW: *Aintree 1979: Monksfield leads Kybo and Sea Pigeon (who is falling)*

The next year, not yet fully recovered from his severely broken leg, Jonjo could only watch the 'poetry in motion as John Francome gave him a gem of a ride, saving him until fifty yards from the line and then simply popping his nose in front of Daring Run and winning by a length and a half from Pollardstown, who took second place near the line. Sea Pigeon did not even know he had had a race under John's cool artistry.' Sea Pigeon died in 2000 at the age of thirty.

In January 2001, Istabraq became the first equine National Hunt millionaire. Two months later, the cruel outbreak of foot-and-mouth disease in Britain prevented him from leaving Ireland and denied him the chance of becoming the first horse ever to win four Champion Hurdles.

Istabraq, by Sadler's Wells out of a Secretariat mare, was also bred to win a Derby. When he failed to live up to expectations on the Flat, there was one young man determined that this

PREVIOUS PAGE: *Leopardstown, Eire, 1999 (left to right) Istabraq (Charlie Swan up), French Holly (Adrian Maguire up)*

LEFT: *J.P. McManus*

should be the horse to set him on his way as a new National Hunt trainer. John Durkan, the son of a successful Irish builder who had also owned and trained Arkle Chase winner Anaglogs Daughter, was hooked on racing from a young age. He rode 100 winners as an amateur, including one each for the Queen and the Queen Mother. He was an assistant trainer in Lambourn, where he led a lively lifestyle along with other bachelor jockeys, and Newmarket. In 1994, he married the successful Irish amateur rider Carol Hyde, who was also in England.

When he set about becoming a trainer in 1996, John Durkan managed, with a combination of determination and persuasion,

BELOW: *Monksfield leads Sea Pigeon in the Champion Hurdle, Cheltenham, 1980*

to acquire not only Istabraq, but also J.P. McManus as his owner; he predicted his new equine acquisition would win the Sun Alliance Novices Hurdle over 2 miles 5 furlongs at Cheltenham. J.P. McManus, an Irish tax exile who lives in Switzerland and Barbados, made his money through betting and trading in international currencies, and keeps many horses in training. He was an excellent owner for John Durkan to have wooed, and the young trainer was on the threshold of his career. Then he fell ill.

Istabraq was sent to Aiden O'Brien to be trained by him temporarily until John Durkan was well enough to carry on again. It was not to be. Stricken with leukaemia, he was able to see Istabraq fulfil his prediction of winning the 1997 novices hurdle at Cheltenham. But in January 1998, two months before Istabraq's first Champion Hurdle victory, John Durkan died. He was thirty-one years old.

In March 2000, Istabraq won his third Champion Hurdle. It was his twenty-first win from twenty-four hurdle runs; he was partnered in every one of them by Charlie Swan, a trainer still hurdle riding as long as Istabraq continues to race. Beaten by a head in his first run over timber in November 1996, Istabraq then set up a sequence of ten wins, including his first Champion Hurdle, before suffering a head defeat again, this time over $2^1/_2$ miles at Aintree, at the hands of A.P. McCoy on Pridwell. The real turn up came at Fairyhouse in November 1999, when, after another sequence of eight wins, including his second Champion Hurdle, Istabraq, at 7–1 on, was beaten by Limestone Lad, who set up a long lead in the $2^1/_2$ -mile race.

Istabraq's next three wins included his third Irish Champion Hurdle and his third Champion Hurdle at Cheltenham. He did not reappear until New Year's Eve, 2000, at Leopardstown, Ireland's smart course just outside Dublin, when he was already ante-post odds-on for a fourth Champion Hurdle. To the horror of his legions of supporters, he fell heavily at the last flight. He had always been a superb jumper and outstandingly consistent. Like a true champion, he gave 100 per cent each time, and, in the hands of Charlie Swan, could 'switch off' until his rider pressed the button.

ABOVE: *Charlie Swan celebrates winning the Champion Hurdle on Istabraq, Cheltenham, 2000*

No one knew for sure how the fall had affected him. Before he next ran, Istabraq could, for about twenty-four hours, be backed at odds-against for the 2001 Champion Hurdle. He has always been a horse about whom rumours and counter-rumours as to his welfare or soundness abound, and this was no exception. Luckily, Istabraq does not know about these things.

On 21 January 2001, it was back to Leopardstown for a crack at a record-breaking fourth Irish Champion Hurdle. J.P. McManus flew in from Barbados, and paid for five coachloads of supporters to drive up from Tipperary to see their hero redeem his reputation. The bright bay horse with the big white star did not fail them: his jumping was impeccable, and his victory was greeted with huge cheers. With that result, he had topped £1 million in prize-money won, a record for a National Hunt horse.

From Point to Point

Spring is in the air. The hamper is packed and bundled into the car boot along with wellies, booze, binoculars and Barbours. All are abuzz about the local point-to-point. Will old so-and-so be trying to win the hunt race again this year?

The North Hereford Hunt point-to-point, 1975

hey say such-and-such has a crack new ex-chaser to run between the flags and rumours surround the amount of purchase money paid for him. Will that old grey, a winner here on this twisting, undulating course for the last four years, still be able to fend off the young bloods?

In the last two decades of the twentieth century, in particular, an element of professionalism crept in to point-to-pointing, yet that is a slur as old as the sport itself. True, there are now professional training yards, reams of red tape, increased Jockey Club regulations and relaxation of the strictly amateurs-only riding

rules. Nevertheless, it remains one of the most truly amateur sports, where participants really are in it for fun, sportsmanship, perhaps glory, but definitely not money. How could they be when the maximum first prize remains at £250?

Point-to-pointing and steeplechasing shared a single birth, in the hunting fields of both Ireland and Britain, where riders pitted their hunters against each other over a line of country from one church steeple to another point in the distance, with only a few marker flags along the way as route guides. In the nineteenth century, as steeplechasing began to evolve round made-up courses, point-to-pointing maintained its tradition across natural country, so it is from this time that point-to-point-

BELOW: *Pat Tollit on Pensham at Garthorpe, 1971*

ing can be identified as a separate entity from steeplechasing. In particular, it remained, and remains, a requirement that a point-to-pointer has been 'regularly and fairly hunted' before it can run in a point-to-point. In 1882, the National Hunt Committee, whose formation in 1866 had saved steeplechasing from going to the dogs, brought in a set of rules for 'racing between the flags' to distinguish it from steeplechasing.

In 1889, fearing competition to the professional cousin, the Committee barred point-to-point organisers from charging gate money, and at the same time prize-money for point-to-points was set at a maximum of £20. Incredibly, this figure was not altered until 1961, when it was 'doubled' (not accounting for inflation) to £40 for an open race and £30 for others. Now, in 2001, £250 may be distributed in an open race, and £175 in others. Additionally, one designated race per area may run a 'prestige' race with up to £500 in prize-money, with a maximum of £250 for first prize.

Between the two world wars point-to-pointing adopted more regulated courses, although there were a few, notably in Northamptonshire, which still contained natural hedges, timber and ditches. One of the main reasons for turning point-to-point tracks into replica steeplechase courses, albeit slightly smaller and for amateurs only, was to improve viewing for spectators who naturally wanted to be able to see for themselves the fate of the mounts on which they had wagered. Racing over banks continued in Cornwall, at least in the hunt members' races, until as recently as 1964; one of the most notable horses over banks was a tiny mare called Delilah, who won forty-eight times between 1954 and 1961. The High Peak in Derbyshire still runs its members' race entirely over stone walls.

An experiment to include cross-country members' races during the 1970s and 1980s failed largely due to the lack of betting interest. Yet, paradoxically, Cheltenham, the premier steeplechase course, now has its own cross-country course, of artificially made fences, for the international Sporting Index Chase held twice a year, and this is proving popular. Some hunts still hold old-fashioned cross-country races, usually referred to

as a 'ride' or 'scurry' so that it cannot be confused with an official race. These are held separately from the point-to-point, and no betting is allowed. The best known is the Melton Hunt Ride in Leicestershire each November, where only about three marker flags are placed, and it is run very much as those early ventures were, with most of the participants being hunters or team chasers.

Between 1930 and 1967, ladies were banned from riding against men (though not in Ireland), and until 1962 they were

BELOW: *Pip Jones on Dawn's Cognac at an Army point-to-point, Larkhill, 2001*

confined to adjacent hunts ladies' races, so most women could take part in a maximum of six or seven races per year. Ladies' open races were introduced in 1963, which gave them one opportunity per meeting, and from 1967, if so allowed by the local committee, they could also ride in their own hunt race. But the Sex Discrimination Act of December 1975 changed all that.

At a stroke, they could ride not only against men in point-to-points, but also under National Hunt Rules. In 1995, Polly Curling rode forty winners in one season.

The great majority of point-to-points are run by individual hunts and consist usually of six races run twice around a 1½ mile circuit with birch fences of 4ft 3in – only three inches lower than the National Hunt minimum – and including an open ditch. The point-to-point provides a 'thank you' to the farmers over whose land the hunt has been allowed during the season, and it does much to swell the hunt's coffers. It is manned almost entirely by volunteers. Conveniences may be on the scant side, but camaraderie amongst point-to-point enthusiasts is great; also, they can roam around freely, without being confined

ABOVE: *Alison Dare on Fennelly at The South Hereford, 1990*

to set enclosures as when racing under National Hunt Rules. They will find favourite old horses from former years still competing, and they will wag their heads knowingly when they see the good jockeys again.

Going back to the 1930s, stalwarts included Major Harold Rushton, whose O'Dell won forty races, including two Liverpool Foxhunters. His daughter, Pat Tollit, was one of the finest lady riders. Yorkshireman Major Guy Cunard and his lovely white-faced Puddle Jumper won many races in the 1960s; the major rode 251 point-to-point winners and was champion rider six times, initially in 1949 and finally in 1964. The major was a strong character who held firm views and was not afraid to expound them, and the sport benefited from men such as he.

One of the very best jockeys was David Tatlow, champion from 1965 to 1968, a great hunting man and one of the country's best show riders. Mystery Gold was a prolific winner, but David had the talent to produce victory from almost any horse. As good as any jockey over the years is the 1999 champion Julian Pritchard, who won forty-three times from an incredible 140 rides in one season. One of my early memories is of the yellow colours with a black 'H' belonging to Guy Harwood, riding horses such as Spinster's Folly to victory in Sussex. Guy went on to become one of the country's best Classic flat race trainers.

The most prolific winning horse between the flags in the last century, and probably of all time, was the tiny Lonesome Boy, who won sixty-five races in the West Country, fifty-three of them consecutively. Hard Frost in East Anglia was another of the period who won thirty-eight of his forty-nine races for George Barber. From Scotland, Flying Ace lived up to his name for Doreen Calder, and in the 1980s joined the select band of horses to have topped a half century of wins, fifty-nine in all, including twenty-two hunter chases. The last horse to do so under National Hunt Rules was Crudwell, between 1949 and 1960.

Point-to-point riders vary from the 'amateur amateur', who has a 'bump round' in his annual hunt race on his own horse, to those who ride out daily, are probably paid 'expenses' by the

ABOVE: *Major Guy Cunard on Puddle Jumper, winning at the Middleton, 1961*

point-to-point trainer and have ridden many winners. In between the two are those who work in an office all week, go to the gym during their lunch breaks and ride at weekends, and for whom the culmination of many months of hard work comes in the local point-to-points – sometimes in the winner's enclosure.

Some point-to-pointers can be purchased for a high price, but it is not possible to buy success; the horse has to remain sound, jump, stay and keep its rider on board. Many bargains picked up with an 'if' at public auction can benefit from the tender loving

care of a small informal yard and go on to win on the point-to-point circuit. Most rewarding of all is the horse bred by the owner, who is often the jockey and trainer as well. Point-to-pointing is still a sport where the true amateur can take on, and beat, the professional at his own game.

The annual point-to point has not changed so much since my first visits in the early 1950s when, at the age of four, the unwavering desire to one day ride in a point-to-point first fired me. Little girls wore jodhpurs to point-to-points in those days, and I remember standing by the open ditch at the old West Kent course at Ightham when a man, who looked very old, asked teasingly if I was riding in the ladies' race.

'No, but I will one day.' Thanks to Rough Scot and Roman Receipt, I won on that very course three times.

Some of the best moments in my life came in point-to-pointing, enriched throughout by the superbly loyal support of my late parents, Rex and Margaret. Many regard the lion-hearted iron grey Rough Scot, who won sixteen races, as their best horse, but before him there was Tarkaotter and the day we travelled him from East Sussex to Dorset in an old trailer.

A mid-air collision had seen me grounded at the first fence at Tweseldown the previous week, and another fall at home in mid-week did not much help my nerves. On the long journey winding down the A272 and beyond, we were stopped by a motorist who told us that the trailer was on fire: the horse was so nervous that he was awash with sweat and steam.

At length we reached Badbury Rings, declared, changed, weighed out, saddled up and mounted for the Wilton Hunt Ladies' Open (it was 1969, before they were any mixed sex races). The course at Badbury Rings is set in a renowned beauty spot below an Iron Age hill fort, the steep hill between the two acting as a natural grandstand for spectators. As I cantered down this hill towards the start, the old horse's stride lengthened, he took a strong hold of the bit and, with a sinking feeling, I realised he was getting the better of me. My legs turned to jelly and my arms were as useless as overcooked spaghetti, but I managed to circle him in the plough and head back towards the runners by now waiting at the start. Tarkaotter stopped so abruptly when he reached the other horses that I fell off like a sack of potatoes. Once I was back in the saddle, Tarka was held in behind the others.

'Has she ever ridden before?' the starter enquired understandably.

'Just jump one fence and pull up,' someone kindly advised.

Pull up! Tarka had no such intention. It took him all of three

fences to weave his way through the rows of equine bottoms and reach the front. He never saw another horse thereafter, and won the race in spite of the fact that he had a complete passenger on top.

Today the sport is flourishing. Some 4,000 horses take part in the point-to-point season that starts in mid-January and ends in early June; that is as many horses as are running under National Hunt Rules throughout the year. It is still the nursery school for future chasers, and a retirement home for old or failed ones, although not all point-to-point races are necessarily easier than those under Rules. The majority of point-to-pointers are just that; they spend their whole working life in the sport with, perhaps, the odd foray into hunter chases. One of the advantages to point-to-pointing is that there is no handicapping, just some penalties and allowances. This means favourites often win, and keep winning for years, so that they become firm friends with the crowds, too.

In the last half of the twentieth century, there were some truly wonderful point-to-pointers, thrilling loyal crowds for years. I am thinking more about horses like Mandryka and Balisteros than See More Business, who went on to win the Cheltenham Gold Cup of 1999. Other subsequent Gold Cup winners were Four Ten in 1954 (ridden to three of his four point-to-point victories by one of the sport's stalwarts, Percy Tory from Dorset); Linwell in 1957; The Dikler in 1973; Norton's Coin in 1990; and Cool Dawn in 1998. The latter's owner, the Hon. Dido Harding, set up a sequence between the flags in the best amateur tradition before being persuaded to allow her horse to run under National Hunt Rules.

Among those whose careers began in point-to-points and who went on to win the Grand National are Teal (1952), Merryman (1960), Highland Wedding (1969), Ben Nevis (1980) and Grittar (1982). We must also salute the many top jockeys who began their careers in point-to-points, such as Bob

LEFT: *David Tatlow on Mystery Gold II, winning at the Beaufort, 1966*

Champion, Peter Scudamore, Bob Davies, Richard Dunwoody, Carl Llewellyn, Hwyel Davies, Robert Thornton and Joe Tizzard, to name but a few. Many top trainers also began by riding in point-to-points: Ian Balding on the Flat, and Robert Alner, Richard Lee and many others in National Hunt racing, including Martin Pipe, who rode one point-to-point winner.

Mandryka was an improbable Welsh star of the 1970s. Barely 15 hands high, little more than a pony, his rider wore a motorcycle helmet on his first ride (much stricter rules do not allow

LEFT: *Anne Holland (author) on Rough Scot at Garthorpe, 1970*

BELOW: *Doreen Calder on Flying Ace, going to the start at Stratford*

ABOVE: *Josie Turner on Sable Lane, winning at the Essex Union, 1967*

such apparel today). A failed hurdler, Mandryka cost just 120 guineas at public auction, but his point-to-point career spanned nearly a decade, with numerous wins, many of them for Shan Morgan in ladies' races. He contested some big hunter chases, including the Cheltenham Foxhunters, but his tiny size was against him; although he won one or two hunter chases, his métier was between the flags.

In the year 2000, the leading point-to-point horse was Balisteros, a 'cast-off' from the all-conquering Richard Barber yard responsible for producing See More Business, among others. Balisteros has thrived in the intimate Scottish yard of Mrs Billie Thomson in Berwickshire and ran on no fewer than seventeen occasions in 2000, winning thirteen times in ten point-to-points and three hunter chases, showing tremendous strength and tenacity. He is a fine example of the sporting, amateur spirit that point-to-pointing encapsulates, and proof positive of the benefit of a small, less regimented yard.

That is not to say that a big, successful yard is not also sporting. Richard Barber, a Dorset farmer, began by running one or two of his own horses, and then one or two for a long-time friend. They were successful, and more owners, those who did not have the time or inclination to do it themselves, asked him to train for them, and so it grew. Richard prepares, schools and trains his horses extremely well and deserves success.

In the 1970s, the yard that was consistently winning (and still is) was that of Joe Turner in East Anglia. His son, David, holds the all-time record for point-to-point wins with 343. His sister, Josie Sheppard, rode 173, bettered only by probably the best lady

BELOW: *The 1973 point-to-point dinner. With their awards (left to right) John Thorne (Special Award), Richard Miller (Leading Man), Mabel Forrest (Leading Lady) and Joe Turner (Leading Horse Owner)*

rider of all time, Alison Dare, with 280 wins (and still riding), Polly Curling with 220, and Pip Jones, also still riding, with 200. Among the superb point-to-pointers produced by the Turners were multiple winners such as Hardcastle, Culford Cottage, Boy Bumble, Even Harmony and Master Vesuvius. Three decades on, Joe Turner is still a leading point-to-point owner, only now it is his grandchildren who are riding with zest. It is this family involvement that is such a fine tradition in the sport.

Easter weekend is traditionally the busiest for point-to-points. This is when crowds big enough to make many National Hunt courses envious turn out to enjoy the banter, the bets and the picnics. There was one Easter weekend when my brother, Tim Holland, my sister, Patsy Smiles, and I won all our respective hunt members' races, a memorable family occasion, especially for our mother. This is the spirit of point-to-pointing that is still very much alive and well today.

'A Demi-god for a Few Hours': Military Races

Hunting and steeplechasing between them helped to make the cavalry a great fighting force. The thrills and spills of the chase gave young men not only prowess in the saddle, but also the ability to think quickly, to adapt to changing situations and to observe both the terrain and the men around them – in short, leadership qualities that are much needed in war.

Special Cargo ridden by Gerald Oxley, winner of the Grand Military Gold Cup, Sandown, 1986

The first military steeplechase is said to have taken place near Newcastle-upon-Tyne in 1804 between two officers of the 5th Light Dragoons. More military races took place near Dublin in 1834, put on by the 5th Dragoon Guards, and later a Grand Military meeting was established at Punchestown in Co. Kildare.

ABOVE: *Columbus, ridden by Captain Charles Lane, winner of the Grand Military Gold Cup, 1988*

England's first Grand Military meeting was staged over three days in Northampton in 1841; it moved to various venues, including Cheltenham, Aintree, Wetherby, Brixworth and Warwick, before settling at Sandown in 1887. It has remained there ever since, and is the pinnacle of the racing soldier's year.

The 1880s and 1890s were the heyday for amateur and soldier riders. The great Cloister, one of the best Grand National winners, started his career as a soldier's horse. After the First World War, there were numerous races staged by the British Army on the Rhine, and soldiers were likely to stage races wherever in the world they were stationed. Between the world wars, numerous bona fide military meetings sprang up around barracks, including Tweseldown near Aldershot, Windmill Hill near Tidworth and Hawthorn Hill in Devon, where the Household Brigade staged meetings.

The handwritten account which follows is of a military steeplechase that took place in Co. Cork in 1860 and was found inside that year's blackened silver trophy by Tom Helme, who lives in Wiltshire, when it was passed on to him by his father. The account was written by his great-great-grandfather, Arthur Thomas Helme. It evokes the lifestyle of the military gentry in the mid-nineteenth century (some of which has barely changed) and graphically describes not only the race itself, but also the build-up to it. The ink handwriting has, in a few places, been impossible to decipher. Modern spelling and grammar have been added.

The Fermoy Military Steeplechase, 25th April 1860. Won by Murphy, ridden by his owner, A. T. Helme, Esq. 95th Regiment
Saturday 21st
How I always bless Saturday when I think, as I lie peacefully in bed, that there is no parade or early drill. I was aroused from my slumbers by White bringing in some splendid trout, a present from Baldwin, so I immediately send to ask Mr Bright to breakfast with me, which he does and, after tomatoes and trout which Mrs Cappayes cooked, I dress. We find that it is about twelve, so

ABOVE: *The silver trophy belonging to Tom Helme, alongside his great-great-grandfather's original handwritten account of a military steeplechase in 1860*

I go and do my morning gallop twice round (three miles), farther than usual, and my spirits rise in proportion; this is Saturday and Wednesday next is the day.

After my ride, I sojourn down with Bright to do the calls, calling by the by on Mrs Chapple (of ours) who is without exception the most affected vulgar piece of humanity it ever was my lot to meet. Mess very full – great excitement about the coming event. Did a little of the old port after dinner as our stock laid in at Mrs Reid's death is almost exhausted and we shall have to come back to the strong black military ditto, which is a caution. The anteroom very noisy as the cards of the race have just come out. We go over to Smith's room and Jardine and Douglas play and sing, the former beginning at 10 with Italian operatic airs and ending at 12.30 with 'Billy Barlow' and variations of 'Harry the Brave'. NB Assistant Surgeons are not much good after 11pm. Turn in at 12.30, sleep like a top.

Sunday 22nd

Thanks to my not drinking spirits, I wake like a bird at 7, tumble into a tub, and do my morning gallop twice round. See Ginger Cordial training hard. Get back in time for parade. Go to church with the men, then a big breakfast with Bright and Smith in briefing room. We then go down to the mufti church, and get in barracks about 2, when we do a walk up the Bafhealy road with a perfect troop of dogs which get worse every day – nearly killed three chickens and worried one goat into a state of apoplexy. Heard from Robert, who seems very jolly, also dear old Pirdre who is more taken up with [. . .] than ever. Bed early.

Monday 23rd

Up at 7, ride with Smith. Now the breeding tells; the little mare walked away from us after two miles and a half, leaving my friend Murphy rather licked. Looks very fishy for Wednesday.

Get back. Thank the rain, no early parade. Smith sports me breakfast and, not liking to offend him, try and eat, though he won't hear reason and believe I had just finished my own breakfast; he nobbles me giving all my food to Nick under the table. Parade at 11 and Chief's drill. Got on well and we tackled him about the exam; he still puts it off, though is beginning to confess we are for it. Go down to see about hiring a vehicle for Wednesday – Sent Sewell who pretends to be in a funk [. . .] to order a hearse to go in, but the idea does not strike Smith, who thinks would be more appropriate to come back in.

Parade again at 2 and Adjutant's drill. Charlton excited about the ball, sending out invitations, etc. Go for a long walk with Mrs Beck and sister in the afternoon, and they kindly offer me a luncheon and a seat in their carriage for Wednesday. My [. . .] is completed and is very swell. Tassell delighted, says the woman who made it must have been a real creature, which is intended for a compliment.

Tuesday 24th

Up at 7. Long & Jock, also Smith & myself in saddle and out for our last sweat, or as Long's groom said, we might try and treat them, which was true in this instance as Red Rover did his three miles without turning a hair. Smith's thoroughbred also well up, [but] to my intense horror Murphy did not go as usual, and the betting went down on me accordingly as the retinue of grooms, helpers, etc. were there in great force. However, as I neither expected I could win nor bet on myself or anyone else, it did not take away my appetite. After that, great drill ensued and then $1^1/_2$-hour examination from the Chief, who was so pleased that he sent our names in there and then, so now I may go up any day for the next three weeks – busy days.

Anteroom in a fever of excitement about tomorrow. Lots flying about everything, and everybody discussed fiercely, and Red Rover going up – sweepstakes etc. – Howard comes in

BELOW: *'Avant La Course' by Auguste de Molins (1810-1886)*

very late with a broken nose and informs us that he found out the farmer to whom the course belongs, and then this farmer took him round as far as he could, for in three jumps his mare came down three times, and he declared it was a barbarous affair and scratched forthwith. The Stewards have had large correspondence with the elite of County Cork and the whole assemblage are going to honour us. Go to bed.

Wednesday. The Day.

Rather excited. Did not sleep long. Woke up at 8. Long day. Parade at 9, all right at 11. Good breakfast. At 12 o'clock went to dress, had no tops [top boots], but Long had had his beautifully cleaned for me and my colours were perfection. But alas, as usual I had left everything to the last, and my leg was much too big for Long's tops. No power on earth would induce my calf to

A Grand Military Steeplechase at Sandown Park in 1890, artist unknown

squash up enough. Did not know what to do. Old Parks came to the rescue and I got one of his on which stopped the circulation and five fellows had to take it off playing a regular game of French & English with me. It was a hell and I had to go in my old Butcher boots, which did not accord with the rest of my get-up. I started for Beck's at 12.45 with his riders Baldwin & Sewell, and a great luncheon awaited us. Only took one glass of champagne. In the middle of lunch I was called out, and I found Captain Montgomery. Having heard of my disappointment about the boots, he most kindly offered to lend me his; he had taken so much trouble, which after his seventeen years' service was more than I could possibly have expected as I knew so little of him, but I was again doomed to disappointment and split one of his boots to pieces. NB My calves are too big for my size.

At 2 we started in a large open carriage, postilion and everything correct. Beck and his wife and her sister, Baldwin, Sewell & myself. After a very jolly drive, we at length reach the course, and I must say the first sight of it rather astonished my weak nerves. I knew all the swells were coming, but for the awful assemblage of carriages, cars, queer looking four-in-hands, inside cars, outside cars, donkey cars, mule cars, every description of conveyance, and post boys who looked as if their clothes were put on after a long rest and did not seem at all comfortable in their respectable jackets. Everyone who kept a horse or donkey within ten miles of this were there and more besides – soldiers without end. The first thing we (the jockeys) did was to walk round the course and a deuced ugly one it was. People all declared it was as bad a course as they ever saw, but we were in for it and the only way was to make the best of it – we had to go twice round 1¼-miles, including twenty-six jumps in the 2½ miles. The second jump was the most beastly of the lot, very high and impossible to clear without topping it, and at first, when horses are not in their stride, it's not easy to get them to see it in the same light. After a great deal of preliminary bothering [. . .], eight of us cantered to the post, and great swells we looked. I could not help feeling a great confidence in Murphy; he was in great condition and with his mane plaited and his swell [forelock braided], and his placid swagger when I mounted felt very jolly; but when looking at the horses I had to contend with I felt it was absurd. Beck's two horses look high priced animals; the horse, a proper thoroughbred, looked very much the winner, and the mare a perfect picture of symmetry and beauty. Long's horse again was a steeplechase [who] has won several races, while little Cox, his rider, has ridden in several also. Long did not believe it possible that Red Rover could be licked and looked very proud of him. Then comes Major Daniell's Ginger Cordial, who has won lots of races, as ugly a brute as could be seen, but the country people seemed to spot him for the winner. Old Daniell's looking greener and more horsey than ever. He makes a deal more money in horse dealing than he does in being Barrack Master. Lastly, the beautiful mare of Captain Smith, but she is excited and he is nervous, so things no good.

For a wonder we start capitally without any false attempts; we walk in a line, past the flag when he drops his hat, and away we go. Ginger Cordial runs away but in the right direction, and the rest of us come to the first fence together. We clear it and for a wonder all arrive in safety on the right side. By this time I feel at home, [with] Murphy going wonderfully. Knowing I can rely on his safety, [I] let him out to his speed and get up to Ginger Cordial, and we make for the fourth fence, a stone wall, together. The last thing I see is Bishop falling on the stones, and on giving a glance round see Billy and Sewell on the ground together. We now get to the eighth fence ahead, but Beck's thoroughbred, ridden beautifully [by] G. Baldwin, comes a stride before me and we make for a large bank overgrown with yellow furze. [His] horse baulks and I again land on the right side the leader, alone. Now it gets select, and coming past the stand the first time I am about sixty yards ahead, then lays Red Rover, then Ginger Cordial after two falls. More falls ensue, Sewell getting three, Smith two and Bishop two, in all making seven falls in the race. I, much to the surprise of myself and everyone, keep up the pace, Murphy not having made one mistake, and come in the winner.

LEFT: *The Queen Mother with the Royal Artillery Gold Cup, Sandown, 2001*

Here I get rather confused as I was perfectly enveloped in a crowd of 1,000 men, women, soldiers, children, officers, and servants, [. . .] and shaken hands with and cheered, [. . .]. At last Charlton seizes me and I am borne away in triumph to Mrs Young, the Judge's wife, who presents me with the cup; and then it is filled with champagne and she drinks, and I drink, and we all drink, and the crowd roar and bellow at the top of their healthy lungs, which lasts a long time as pretty speeches from all the fellows, great cheering from all the crowds, besides vociferous [. . .] and trying to lift me off my hind by the 95th Soldiers present. I tried to answer my pretty speeches with ditto, utterly failing as my wind had entirely disappeared, and there I was as

like a fool [. . .] till I took a great rush and got into the carriage and even then the people would come and cheer. After this a race is made on the ground; £7 is collected, which Beck wins, his servant riding, but this is impromptu and Murphy was sent home directly after the great event. The Cup is very pretty, 10 guineas worth of good silver, and has gone to Cork today to have an inscription on it, which is to be: 'Fermoy Military Steeplechase, 25th April 1860. Won by Murphy, ridden by his owner, A.T. Helme, Esq. 95th Regiment.'

And so the great event is over and I am a sort of demi-god for a few hours – Tassell's delight exceeds my own and he requests me to write to Broadfield instantly.

An American Import:

Timber Racing

'Having imported steeplechasing from England, we welcome the chance to give a little back in the form of timber racing.' Thus spoke American Arthur W. 'Nick' Arundel, founder and president of Great Meadow Timber Racecourse, Virginia, venue of the Virginia Gold Cup, during the preliminaries of the Marlborough Cup, Britain's only timber race, in 2000.

Linton Rocks, winner of the Marlborough Cup, 2000, ridden by Joe Tizzard

merica's oldest and most famous timber race is the Maryland Hunt Cup, run every April over solid upright rails, some of them five feet high, at Worthington, Maryland. Hunting of some form or another had been going on since the first colonists settled in the area. In 1649, Robert Brooke was appointed by Lord Baltimore as a member of the 'Privy Council of State within our said Province of Maryland'. Brooke created De La Brooke plantation, covering 2,000 acres of what is now Queen Anne County, and arrived in 1650 with his wife, eight sons, two daughters, twenty-eight servants – and a pack of hounds. One of the requirements for immigrant families was that they bring one dog with them. To begin with the dogs were used for protection and for 'pot hunting', but as life became easier for the settlers, they began to acquire a little leisure time, and what better to do than to start up a few packs of hounds?

ABOVE: *Pennybridge (Marlborough Cup winner in 1999) finished 2nd in 2000 (ridden by Richard Johnson)*

The origin of timber racing almost mirrors that of steeple-chasing. In 1894, a group of hunting gentlemen begin discussing the relative merits of their hunters. The conversation becomes somewhat heated and there is only one time-honoured way to resolve the issue: to stage a cross-country race to establish which horse is best. The result was the first running of the Maryland Hunt Cup, a competition between two vying hunts, the Elkridge Club (since 1934, the Elkridge-Harford Hunt, following a merger), and the Green Spring Valley Hounds.

It was to be run over four miles of natural country, flagged at intervals. There was already in existence some English-style steeplechasing over made-up courses, but this race was to have

ABOVE: *Uncle Merlin, eventual winner (left), ridden by P. Neilson, and Ballybranogue, ridden by B. Hannum, at the Maryland Hunt Cup, 1989*

no artificial jumps. A race run in a more or less straight four miles parallel to the road, enabling it to be seen easily from on horseback or by buggy, appealed to spectators early on. Today, it is the social event of the year in Maryland. Those viewers of that first running were able to see the field of nine representing the two hunts tackle some big fences, including an in-and-out reminiscent of Ireland's early boreens, a deep ford and the last, which was said to be a 4ft 10in board fence with a wide ditch.

The victor, in heavy ground, was a horse called Johnny Miller who, in a slog over the last half mile, overhauled first Sixty and then the long-time leader, Tim Burr. Johnny Miller was owned, trained and ridden by John McHenry, representing the Green Spring Valley Hunt. The race was such an undoubted success among the large and enthusiastic crowd that by the end of the day it had been agreed to make the Maryland Hunt Cup an annual race.

For its first ten years, the race was open only to fox-hunting gentlemen in Maryland, but in 1903, in recognition of its growing status and reputation, it was opened to members of hunt clubs anywhere in the United States and Canada. None participated until 1909, when horses from Pennsylvania dominated the race and continued to do so for the next few years.

In 1906, when thoroughbreds by then well outnumbered half-breds, previous winning owners and riders asked the organising committee that the course be the same each year, that

certain weight allowances be made and that prize-money be offered along with the cup. Only the latter request was turned down out of hand; weight allowances were given to young horses, and the committee said they were looking for a permanent course. In 1922, Worthington Valley, where the race had been held from 1915 to 1918, became its official venue. Worthington Valley has no grandstands, but spectators gain excellent viewing of the whole course from a hill. The posts and rails fences are either four or five rails high. To stand beside one of these fences is awesome; to approach it at racing pace on a horse is definitely an experience only for the brave. Prize-money of $6,000 was eventually introduced in 1972. It now stands at $65,000, making it the richest race over timber in the United States.

The small fields of mainly hunters had finally become a thing of the past when twenty-three horses lined up in 1915. These horses were mostly thoroughbreds, and most had been hard trained to be racing fit rather than hunting fit, as befitted a course that by then was all permanent pasture with no plough or wheat, no rivers to ford and no ditches. Board fences and awesome timber remained, as they have to the present day, and they are what has made the race so famous.

Jay Trump and Ben Nevis, winners of the Maryland Hunt Cup, are heroes who have gone on to win the Grand National. Jay Trump was all American, but Ben Nevis started life running in English point-to-points before joining Charlie Fenwick's stable near Worthington in Maryland. He won the Maryland Hunt Cup in 1977 and 1978, then brought the chestnut back to England twice to contest the National. Ben Nevis was brought down in 1979, but deservedly won in 1980.

Jay Trump began his illustrious career inauspiciously, flogging round quarter-horse dirt tracks. At two years old, he had been cut so badly by a piece of tin that he nearly died, and

LEFT: *Ben Nevis, ridden by Charlie Fenwick, winner of the Grand National, 1980*

he changed hands many times. Fortunately, he was spotted by a dedicated amateur rider, Tommy Crompton Smith, who bought him for $2,000 for owner Mrs Mary Stephenson. She was looking for a Hunt Cup prospect. As part of his preparation for timber racing, Jay Trump was taken hunting twenty-five times with the Green Spring Valley Hounds, gaining him invaluable experience in learning to look after himself and keep his feet in tricky situations. When he first contested the Maryland Hunt Cup at only six years old, he beat the previous year's winner, Mountain Dew, a horse with whom he was to have many battles. Victories and defeats were fairly evenly distributed, except in the Hunt Cup, where the good-looking Jay Trump, pulling hard, won on each occasion he contested it, in 1963, 1964 and 1966. Mountain Dew won in 1962, 1965 (when Jay Trump was away in England) and 1967, after Jay Trump's retirement.

When Jay Trump travelled to England, accompanied by Tommy Crompton Smith, he became Fred Winter's first runner

ABOVE: *Jay Trump, ridden by Tommy Crompton Smith, leading a line of Fred Winter's horses in training at Lambourn, Berkshire*

RIGHT: *The Count and Countess Konrad Goess-Saurau*

and first winner as a trainer. In all, he won three of his five prep races, and was given a copy-book ride at Aintree. Throughout his spell in England, he was not only ridden by Tommy Crompton Smith, but tended by him every waking hour as well. The fledgling staff at Uplands loved the horse, not least because he was so well schooled that he was pure pleasure to have around. Jay Trump returned to America to win the Maryland Hunt Cup one last time in 1966, whereupon, at the age of only nine, he was retired. He lived well into his thirties, cared for by his owner's granddaughter, Serena Stephenson.

As the Maryland Hunt Cup grew in stature from the 1920s, so did timber racing in America. Other races were added to the calendar, notably the Grand National Point-to-Point and the My Lady's Manor, both of which became established prep races for the Hunt Cup. The sport spread, and in 1922 the Virginia Gold Cup was inaugurated but, until recently, it had never been staged 'across the pond' in Britain.

Count Konrad Goess-Saurau has changed that. An Austrian with a bush of dark hair, round, deep eyes and an almost boyish, certain charm, he spent much of his young life in Kenya in the family concrete business. Now married to Susie and settled in England, he established the Marlborough Cup on the downs in Wiltshire in 1995. Six short years later, it was part of a four-race, four-nation Marlborough Million Challenge, along with the Virginia Gold Cup in America, the Grand Cros de Craon in France and the Kevin McManus Punchestown Cup in Ireland.

Count Konrad is a man with a vision, but it is one that came about by chance. Always interested in horses, the count had represented his native country in eventing. As soon as he saw Temple Farm, near Marlborough, he noticed the potential for a racecourse. After all, the illustrious Brown Jack (see p.51), six times winner of the Queen Alexandra Stakes at Royal Ascot from 1929 to 1934 and of the 1928 Champion Hurdle, had been trained there by Aubrey Hastings and, after his death, by Ivor Anthony. The old turf was springy and constant; the downland was excellent for providing the hill work needed to reach peak

fitness; and the setting was glorious. So the initial 2,500 acres was bought by the count's family trust as an investment. Now there are 4,300 acres, taking in Barbury Castle, where Konrad re-established a point-to-point course that had been defunct since 1962.

At the time, Konrad owned a very fast eventer. He was one of those horses who falls between two stools: too headstrong for eventing, but not good enough to be a top-class steeplechaser. It was this horse that set the count to thinking of an alternative type of competition.

'I thought it would be fun to stage a race for amateurs, for some of the crazy, kamikaze British who are real horsemen, a cross somewhere between a horse trial, a point-to-point and a team chase. . . . But I was wrong!' In simple terms, there was not enough support for it.

'Then I saw pictures of the Maryland Hunt Cup; it was fascinating. People here look down on American racing, but the horses jump and they do their job, and to race over even three feet of timber they have to jump, unlike our hurdlers.'

This is something of a bête noire with the count, who is not alone in feeling that hurdle racing encourages horses to jump too fast and flat. The count, like many others, hates seeing the equivalent of 'rapped knuckles' when hurdles 'ping back' into runners, and feels that National Hunt racing is 'in big danger of being hijacked by flat-race rejects, who are not bred to gallop and jump through a foot of mud.'

He adds, 'We don't want 100 mph horses; we need tough, strong mares who can go round the National, but if we are not careful we will lose them.'

On this issue, France, he thinks, is well ahead of Britain, especially in the breeding of chasers. 'They are steaming ahead, because there are cross-country races open to half-breds and they jump like kangaroos. The use of Anglo-Arabs breeds tough, well-limbed, sound horses with stamina who can gallop and jump. After three generations of crossing with thoroughbreds, they are eligible to go chasing. They are breeding much more for future chasers.' The French courses encourage this. A race like the Grand Cros de Craon, the French leg of the World Timber

Championship, is run over thirty-one fences, including banks, ditches, steeplechase fences and timber, covering 3³/₄ miles each September. New Zealand, too, is breeding jumpers, Konrad said.

So, with the idea of an English timber race forming in his mind, Konrad was off to Maryland, accompanied by trainer Kim Bailey and event rider turned permit trainer Ginny Elliot. When there, they met Lucinda Green, the six times Badminton Horse Trials winner, as well as the timber-racing organisers and many enthusiasts.

'The whole social scene is there, with their picnic lunches and lashings of drink. There is only the one race, and the jockeys come out for it like gladiators. Out there, even to own a Maryland Hunt Cup horse is a once in a lifetime dream; to win it, the ultimate. The sport is much smaller. It is the social side which is the big thing.'

Not a few staid eyebrows were raised in response to Konrad's plans, but a handful of well-respected British racing and eventing names supported the idea and helped persuade the Jockey Club to accept them. 'Without Richard Pitman, Ginny Elliot, Hugh Thomas and Ian Balding, it would never have got off the ground,' Konrad conceded. 'I was a nobody and had no hope on my own, but these people have encouraged me throughout and were prepared to put their heads on the block.'

Their credentials were impeccable: Richard Pitman had been a leading National Hunt jockey (who will ever forget his epic ride abroad Crisp in the 1973 Grand National?) and is now a respected television racing commentator, who is always willing to help people behind the scenes. Ginny Elliot was one of the world's leading three-day-event riders, with numerous Olympic, World, European, Badminton and Burghley medals and prizes under her belt. More recently, she has turned her hand to training point-to-pointers and hunts regularly. Hugh Thomas, likewise, was a top-class event rider and has been director of Badminton Horse Trials since 1989. He is also one of the world's leading course designers, responsible not only for Badminton, but also for the 1988 Olympic Games in Seoul,

ABOVE: *Richard Pitman*

South Korea, among others. Ian Balding, apart from being a flat race trainer for the Queen, was a good hunter chase and point-to-point rider, and is a leading light and former Master of the Berks and Bucks Draghounds. It is on his lovely downland near Kingsclere that the draghunt stages its annual team chase – an event Ian still likes to win – and hunter trials. Later, Nick Cheyne, Clerk of the Course at Ascot, joined the timber board in the same capacity for Marlborough.

There was thus a broad mix of jumping experience, both racing and cross-country, to support the application to the Jockey Club. On agreement that there would be qualifying races, run on the inside of the point-to-point course at Barbury

Eventual winner Saluter takes the last fence at the Marlborough Cup, 1997

Castle, as well as observed timber schooling sessions, before any horse could take part in the Marlborough Cup race itself, the venture was finally given the go-ahead.

The particular input from Hugh and Ginny was in the type and construction of fences. Ginny felt horses found it easier to gallop and jump at substantial timber, rather than anything flimsy. The Cup fences stand at 4ft 3in and are sloped (unlike those in the Maryland Hunt Cup which are upright) and are lashed together in sections, as designed by Hugh Thomas, so that if a fence is hit hard, that section should give way rather than bring the horse down. In a further attempt to avoid falls, the last three fences are much smaller, about three feet high, though still built of solid timber. Hugh had visited a number of timber racetracks in America and, with the exception of the Maryland Hunt Cup, found most of the timber rather flimsy and quite small.

The count acknowledges that, with 'the best racing in the world on our doorstep every weekend', and with timber racing as yet barely established in England, it is impossible to put on a full, good race card. Various ideas have been mooted, such as Arab racing or team chasing. The best compromise may have been that reached for the 2001 running when, for the first time, instead of having a prize for the best amateur trained and ridden horse in the Cup, there was to have been a separate, supporting race open only to qualified point-to-pointers and hunter chasers. It was to have been run over the last two-and-a-half miles of the three-mile Marlborough Cup course and would have carried a £10,000 purse, £4,000 of which was to have gone to the winner. The Marlborough Cup remains at £15,000 for the winner from a total prize fund of £30,000. Sadly, the 2001 Marlborough Cup had to be cancelled, as the venue was quarantined for six months following a foot-and-mouth outbreak.

In 1997, the Cup took on an international flavour in only its third running, when Saluter travelled over from America to win for owners Mrs Anne Stern, from Monkton, Maryland, and Jack Fisher, who also rode and trained the gelding. Saluter was favourite the following year, but he uncharacteristically fell when well in contention. In 1999, he could finish only third to Pennybridge, who won in record time under Richard Johnson. Saluter was without doubt one of America's best timber racers and won the prestigious Virginia Gold Cup no less than six times. His retirement was announced early in 2001, the twelve-year-old having amassed $429,489 from his twenty-one American timber victories, the Marlborough Cup bringing his total number of wins to twenty-two.

Pennybridge attempted to repeat his win in 2000, a feat no horse has yet achieved. That year there were several international entries, including Royal Etranger for France, Native Status for the Carberry stable in Ireland and Priceless Room from America. As Priceless Room had won the 2000 Virginia Gold Cup, leaving Saluter in third place and Pennybridge in fourth, he was entitled to be well fancied, but he pulled up at the penultimate obstacle. Poor Royal Etranger fell at the first, but connections of both horses were extremely sporting in defeat. Pennybridge jumped superbly, but although he came with a sustained effort up the long, sweeping final hill, he could not quite catch the Paul Nicholls-trained Linton Rocks. Owned by Charlotte Townsend, a Master of the Cattistock Hunt, he was ridden by Joe Tizzard, who received his grounding in horsemanship in the deep going and over the big black hedges of the Blackmore and Sparkford Vale hunting country in Dorset.

The Marlborough Cup can now truly be said to have come of age. Apart from the keen international competition, Count Konrad Goess-Saurau has achieved his aim of making it the place to be on the last Sunday in May. Spectators arrive loaded with picnics and drinks, countless quality tented shops vie for trade, and there are many supporting county fair types of attractions during the day, as well as a huge charity ball the night before. Clearly the count's dream is beginning to materialise.

The race is a unique sporting challenge in England that has brought a revitalising breath of fresh air. Former cynics come and enjoy what is in many ways an utterly English occasion, despite the fact that it was brought here from America by an Austrian. Above all, the day is about providing fun.

PART TWO
The People
2

Lambourn: trainer Fulke Walwyn's string

The Queen of Steeplechasing: HM Queen Elizabeth the Queen Mother

In 1949, Her Majesty Queen Elizabeth the Queen Mother famously shared a horse, Monaveen, with her daughter, then Princess Elizabeth. While the Queen pursued her racing interest on the Flat, jumping continued as the passion for the Queen Mother.

One Man, ridden by Brian Harding, winner of the Queen Mother Champion Chase, Cheltenham, 1998

Over the next fifty years, her horses won more than 450 races. A royal winner, no matter how modest, is invariably greeted by hats being tossed into the air and plenty of cheers.

Monaveen, ridden by Tony Grantham, was an immediate success, winning several races and placing second in the Grand Sefton over the Aintree fences, making him a Grand National contender. So began the Queen Mother's attempt to win the great race, although in that year, 1950, he wore the Princess Elizabeth's colours. Monaveen, at 50–1, had fallen in the National for his previous owner the year before, but he now had much better form and was not disgraced by finishing fifth in the race won by Freebooter. Sadly, the royal owners were all too soon to see the down side of racing for, when attempting to win a second Queen Elizabeth Chase at the now defunct Hurst Park, Monaveen fell at the water, broke a leg and had to be put down.

Manicou, a full horse who later became a successful stallion, became the Queen Mother's second steeplechaser, after the death in a drowning accident of his former owner, Lord Mildmay, who himself came tantalisingly close to winning the Grand National. At only five years old, Manicou won the King George VI Chase at Kempton Park on Boxing Day, 1950, ridden by Bryan Marshall, who died in February 2001.

So Her Majesty quickly saw both the good and the bad sides of National Hunt racing before she had what were to be her only two blank seasons throughout her half century as an owner. By 1953, she had M'as-tu-vu, who won two races each season for the next three seasons. In 1954, Devon Loch came under her owner-ship, and he also won two races per season for three years in a row. But it is, of course, for the race he didn't win that he is immortally remembered.

I don't really remember Devon Loch's National (my first definite memory of the race is having 6d on Kilmore in 1962),

ABOVE: *The Queen Mother watches the Grand National in 1927*

RIGHT: *The Queen Mother's horse Monaveen, with jockey Tony Grantham in the saddle, trains for the 1950 Grand National which took place the next day*

but I most certainly grew up on the story. And when I was a young member of the Eridge Hunt branch of the Pony Club, I clearly recollect visiting Peter Cazalet's stables at Fairlawne, near Tonbridge in Kent, and being shown 'the horse that didn't win the Grand National'. Another abiding youthful memory of that visit was how spick and span everything was, as well as how grand – it was a magnificent stable yard.

Devon Loch's early promise was interrupted by tendon trouble, which necessitated nearly two years off the racecourse, and ultimately prompted his retirement. In the 1955–6 season, patience was rewarded and the well-bred bay with the big white star showed that he jumped and stayed well. In his novice chase wins he had beaten good horses, and the firm target for spring 1956 was the Grand National.

The Queen Mother had two runners that year, for M'as-tu-vu also ran and led for much of the first circuit. Tucked in mid-division, Devon Loch was giving his jockey, Dick Francis, a dream ride, and jumped his way into second place by the Canal Turn the second time round. Dick Francis was in the unusual

RIGHT: *Devon Loch, ridden by Dick Francis, collapses on the run-in, when leading the 1956 Grand National*

LEFT: *Monaveen (centre) during a training gallop at Hurst Park*

position of having to steady his mount, and over the last two fences he still had a fresh horse, while the remaining runners were all tired. Devon Loch jumped the last perfectly, ears pricked, stretching right over the fence, a weary ESB just behind him.

What caused Devon Loch to sprawl to the ground when level with the water jump on the run-in, victory certain with only those remaining fifty yards to cover, will never be known for sure. What is known is how gracious the Queen Mother was at such a dramatic moment and after. She showed concern for her horse, her jockey, her trainer, the horse's lad – and she charmingly received the winning connections of ESB, trainer Fred Rimell, jockey Dave Dick and owner Mrs L. Carver. She displayed no self-pity and conducted herself with the poise, grace and decorum for which she has become so well loved.

Many of the Queen Mother's winners over the years are still well remembered: Double Star, who won seventeen races for jockeys Dick Francis, Arthur Freeman and Bill Rees between 1956 and

were transferred to Fulke Walwyn at Lambourn, where one of Her Majesty's best horses, Game Spirit, continued to win for the new stable. He won twenty-one races in all, and his third to Captain Christy and The Dikler in the 1974 Cheltenham Gold Cup coincided with the retirement of his rider, the ever-smiling, blond-mopped Terry Biddlecombe.

Colonius, mostly ridden by Bill Smith and Aly Branford, and Isle of Man, who gave Bill Smith his 500th winner, both won fourteen races. Sunyboy gave the Queen Mother her 300th winner in 1976 and became a successful National Hunt stallion. The Argonaut's fifteen wins included many for Stuart Shilston, as well as for amateurs Mark Bradstock and Gerald Oxley.

Fulke Walwyn was justifiably proud that he trained 150 winners for Her Majesty. Among the most popular of these was the Sandown specialist Special Cargo. He won a truly memorable Whitbread Gold Cup of 1984, under Kevin Mooney,

PREVIOUS PAGE: *Cheltenham Festival, 1999*

ABOVE: *Devon Loch, ridden by Dick Francis, leading ESB over the last jump in the Grand National, 1956*

RIGHT: *The Queen Mother and Special Cargo after the Grand Military Gold Cup, Sandown, 1985*

1963, and Silver Dome. The Rip had thirteen wins and a third in the Hennessy Gold Cup; and Laffy had twelve wins and a third in the Whitbread Gold Cup. Makaldar's fifteen wins came mostly under David Mould, the supreme stylist who won more races for the Queen Mother than any other jockey. Makaldar won the Mackeson Hurdle at Cheltenham and the Black and White Gold Cup at Ascot, as well as a second in the Champion Hurdle of 1967 to Saucy Kit. Chaou II, a dapple grey, won seventeen races, mostly for David Mould, and Escalus won nine and was third in the Champion Hurdle. Inch Arran's fourteen wins were mostly for Richard Dennard.

When Peter Cazalet died in 1973, the Queen Mother's horses

and the Grand Military Gold Cup for three successive years, 1984–6, ridden by amateur Gerald Oxley. In one of these races he had a stirrup leather break, leaving him to ride much of the way without stirrups.

Special Cargo, a dark bay, was Fulke Walwyn's second string in the 1984 Whitbread Gold Cup, when his Diamond Edge, who always out-galloped Special Cargo by a street at home, was the horse Bill Smith elected to ride, leaving 'Special' for Kevin Mooney. It proved one of the greatest races ever witnessed at Sandown. Special Cargo flew those railway fences, found a gap on the inside rail and steadily devoured the remaining ground, catching up with Diamond Edge, Lettoch and Plundering from the last fence. It was a four-way finish. The photograph showed Special Cargo had won by a short head from Lettoch, who was also a short head in front of Diamond Edge, but in truth it was more like two nostrils, with Plundering only just notched out of it.

There have not been the big multiple winners in later years for the Queen Mother; nevertheless, a steady stream have found their way to the number one berth, many of them ridden by Mick Fitzgerald for trainer Nicky Henderson. He took over the majority of the Queen Mother's horses following the death of Fulke Walwyn and the retirement of his widow, Cath.

Nearco Bay was the horse who recorded Her Majesty's 400th winner in 1994, ridden by John Kavanagh. For every jockey, professional, conditional or amateur, who has ever won in the famous blue and buff colours with gold tassel, the experience has been a red letter occasion. They exemplify the very high race-riding standards during the second half of the twentieth century.

There are some constants in one's life, and for most of us the Queen Mother has been one of them. I have a Brownie picture of her in the paddock at Sandown when Arkle was parading – possibly the greatest equine and human steeplechasing icons of the twentieth century appropriately together. Arkle, bless him, has been a treasured memory for many years, but we are still privileged to have numerous glimpses of the Queen Mother, especially at Sandown and Cheltenham. Her one concession to

gracious old age has been her chauffeur-driven motorised buggy, painted in her racing colours of blue and buff, and open topped, as ever, so that she can see, as well as be seen. At Sandown on 10 March 2001, the Queen Mother, whose horse Braes of Mar won, like everyone else on arrival, dipped her feet in disinfectant as a precaution against foot-and-mouth disease.

ABOVE: *The Queen Mother, trainer Peter Cazalet and jockey Dick Francis in the unsaddling enclosure with Devon Loch, after his victory in the Sandown Handicap Chase, 1955*

In 1980, the Queen Mother lent her title to the Two Mile Champion Chase, the Cheltenham race which is colloquially now referred to as 'the Queen Mother'. The prefix was a fitting tribute to Her Majesty's eightieth year. While the Cheltenham Gold Cup over $3\frac{1}{4}$ miles is the pinnacle of steeplechasing, the fastest hurdlers and the fastest chasers are recognised in the Champion Hurdle and the Queen Mother Two Mile Champion Chase respectively. The combination of sheer speed over a shorter distance has resulted in some phenomenal jumping and exhilarating finishes over the years.

Set in the beautiful amphitheatre at the foot of Cleeve Hill on

the outskirts of the lovely regency town, Cheltenham is to National Hunt racing what Newmarket is to the Flat. The three most important days in the steeplechasing calendar fall in mid-March for the National Hunt Festival at Cheltenham. Every race is important. The big three of Champion Hurdle (Tuesday), Queen Mother Two Mile Champion Chase (Wednesday) and Thursday's Cheltenham Gold Cup are supported by prestigious novice, handicap and amateur races. Simply to have a runner at the Festival is the height of ambition for many owners.

Tickets are sold out months in advance, as is corporate hospitality. There are acres of marquees forming the tented village

LEFT: *Champion hurdle contender Escalus, ridden by jockey David Mould in 1970*

BELOW: *Badsworth Boy, ridden by jockey Robert Earnshaw, three times winner of the Queen Mother Two Mile Champion Chase*

full of high-class shops and hospitality venues. Every other voice seems to be Irish. There isn't space to move, but the atmosphere is electric. Flat racing at Cheltenham in the nineteenth century did not survive the preachings on the supposed sins of racing and evils of gambling by the Revd (later Dean) Francis Close, but steeplechasing did. The oldest race still run today is the Grand Annual Steeplechase, dating from 1834. Liverpool and the Grand National remained the pinnacle for a century, but with the founding in 1924 of the Cheltenham Gold Cup, won by Red Splash, and in 1927 of the Champion Hurdle, both at level weights, the Festival spirit began to take shape, something that has grown ever since.

Dunkirk and Flyingbolt were exceptional winners of the Two Mile Champion Chase in 1965 and 1966. Flyingbolt, according to his trainer, Tom Dreaper, was positively swanking as he pulled hard in second place before pulling clear to win by six lengths. Incredibly, he turned out again the next day in the Champion Hurdle and very nearly won that, too, going under to Salmon Spray and just pipped for second by Sempervivum.

In the 1970s, the late Edward Courage's home-bred Royal Relief (by Flush Royal out of French Coleen) ran in the race six times during a ten-year career, winning it in 1972 and 1974, remaining sound and retaining his enthusiasm throughout. There were some epic races in the 1980s, when Michael Dickinson's Badsworth Boy won three years in succession, ridden each time by Robert Earnshaw. In the last of his three wins, the odds-on favourite, Bobsline, fell, and Badsworth Boy completed his hat trick with his ears pricked; he thoroughly deserved the accolade 'simply superb'.

The 1990s saw some of the closest and most exciting finishes, involving horses such as Waterloo Boy, Katabatic, Viking Flagship and Deep Sensation, but probably the most popular 'Queen Mother' winner of all was the grey, One Man. A three-mile chaser of the top class, he had twice run in the Gold Cup only to 'hit a brick wall' when faced with that extra quarter mile. In 1998, Cumbrian trainer Gordon Richards ran him instead in the 'Queen Mother', ridden by his second jockey, Brian

Harding, and it was a revelation that was as heartwarming as it was brilliant. The big grey, sporting the yellow colours with red star, simply toyed with the high-class opposition, and jumped the other horses spectacularly into the ground. He was ridden beautifully on the rails and literally sailed over the last fence to gallop home to cheers, and not a few tears, from the Queen Mother included. It was the twentieth, and finest, win of One Man's career. Less than a month later, he fell and died in the Mumm Melling Chase over the Mildmay fences at Liverpool.

ABOVE: *Cheltenham Gold Cup, 1991: Mark Pitman receives his trophy from the Queen Mother*

His trainer, Gordon Richards, a stalwart of the North, died later the same year. And One Man's usual jockey, Richard Dunwoody, three times champion earlier in the 1990s, had his career ended in December 1999 on doctor's orders.

The 'Queen Mother' never fails to produce a steeplechase of the highest order, and invariably Her Majesty presents the trophy afterwards. It is part of the Cheltenham tradition, as is the Queen Mother herself.

Findon Feast and Famine: Ryan Price and Josh Gifford

Josh Gifford, a youthful sixty now, was only eleven

years old when he first rode in a race. His career

in racing, both as four times champion National

Hunt jockey and as a leading National Hunt trainer,

has spanned half a century already.

Bob Champion and Aldaniti jump Becher's Brook for the 2nd time
on their way to a famous victory in the 1981 Grand National

It has included incredible highs, abominable lows and the ultimate fairy story. The son of Tom Gifford, a Lincolnshire farmer who rode 100 point-to-point winners, Josh was ten years old when trainer Cliff Beechener asked him what he wanted to be.

'A jockey,' was the youngster's swift reply.

The very next day, Josh left home, signed on as an apprentice for three years, and effectively finished his formal schooling. Officially, he had a private tutor in Hugo Bevan, who was all of five years older and who also spent his lifetime in racing. He is remembered by National Hunt racegoers as Clerk of the Course to Huntingdon, Towcester, Worcester and Windsor. Hugo's

ABOVE: *Trainer Ryan Price on Musk Orchid at his stables in Findon, West Sussex, 1967*

sixty-fifth birthday was celebrated at Huntingdon on 15 March 2001 with races named after him: 'Hugo Bevan 65 Today is Over the Hill Novice Hurdle'; 'Hobbling Hugo Handicap Hurdle'; 'Happy Birthday Hugo Bevan Chase'; and 'Hugo Bevan Never Flaps Handicap Chase'.

Josh did attend school for a little while, mostly on sports days or when there was cricket or football to be played. An all-round sportsman, Josh is finally relinquishing his cricket bat – what fun he used to have at the Injured Jockeys' Fund match, held annually at Findon – and taking golf a little more seriously instead. He still rides out two lots a day, sometimes three. Josh had 600 rides on the Flat, but as a teenager he moved to The Downs, Findon, West Sussex, to join Captain Ryan Price, for whom 'training maestro' is not an exaggerated title, and has been there ever since.

The stables, established in the nineteenth century, lie snug against the lee of the South Downs, where the centuries-old turf is soft and springy and naturally well drained. It may be cold and windswept in winter, but it imparts a marvellous sense of freedom, of being on top of the world. On a September day in 1983, I met Captain Price there to view his retired racehorses turned out on the downs. Ryan Price was a brilliant rider to hounds, a leading point-to-point rider, a brave commando during the Second World War (he was Montgomery's bodyguard), one of the most talented racehorse trainers and canny with the placing of his horses on behalf of his owners. He was ahead of his time in training perfection and in improving horses, much as Martin Pipe has been more recently. He paid the penalty through jealousy, to the extent of being disqualified for a horse showing 'abnormal improvement'. He held his horses and jockeys – Fred Winter, Josh Gifford, Paul Kelleway – in the highest regard, second only to his wife, Dorothy, and family, and he was utterly straight, in every sense of the word.

He never allowed any of his equine charges to slide down the slippery slope towards oblivion. Instead, they returned to him for a life of freedom on the downs, and on my visit, the youngest of the horses there was an incredible twenty-eight years old.

ABOVE: *Cheltenham Gold Cup winner What A Myth is led into the parade ring after his victory in 1969*

Their names alone tell much of the story of Ryan Price: Le Vermontois, winner of the Schweppes Gold Trophy hurdle at Newbury (now the Tote Gold Trophy) as a maiden; Cesarewitch winner Major Rose; Cheltenham Gold Cup victor What A Myth; Persian Lancer, whom he rated his greatest training feat of them all. And what a feat! Third in the Cesarewitch as a three-year-old when trained by Sir Gordon Richards, he subsequently broke down, was gelded and sent to Captain Price. Five years later, and without a race in between, though all too many mishaps, he won the Cesarewitch for Ryan.

'He was as honest as they come,' he said.

Major Rose won the Cesarewitch under Lester Piggott, and was beaten only half a length by triple title-holder Persian War in the Champion Hurdle. Captain Price eventually bought him

back cheaply at the sales 'with his joints on the floor' and nursed him in his box for six months.

'He's a smashing old horse and a bloody good friend to me,' the captain added.

Ryan had maintained thoughts of hunting the chestnut What A Myth, retired after his Gold Cup win of 1969 when it came up mud – until he saw Josh up-end on him twice! Hill House, another horse he bought back, and Kilmore had also been part of the gang of old heroes to end their days on the Findon downs. They were inspected daily by the captain and fed oats twice a day from August onwards to maintain their body heat.

'The horses have been my life, and the least I can do is offer them decent retirement,' he said. In a typical Price comment, he said, 'I'd rather talk to them than most people I know!' Considering some of the controversy he encountered along the way, that is not surprising.

Ryan, with the great help of Dorothy, began training from a caravan. Hard work and unstinting perfection began to reap their rewards, and together they restored The Downs to the fine jumping centre it had been formerly, when horses such as Jerry M and Covertcoat were sent out by Robert Gore to win the consecutive Grand Nationals of 1912 (the year Ryan Price was born) and 1913 (see p.44). To begin with, Ryan mostly won sellers and modest races round the southern tracks of Wye, Folkestone, Plumpton and Fontwell. Each August he would make a foray on the West Country holiday meetings.

His commitment, flamboyancy and the gradual increase in the number of winners he produced attracted more and wealthier owners and with them the prestige races: three Champion Hurdles (Clair Soleil in 1955, Fare Time in 1959 and Eborneezer in 1961); the Grand National (Kilmore in 1962) – all ridden by Fred Winter; and the Cheltenham Gold Cup (What A Myth in 1969, ridden by Paul Kelleway). But it is for his domination of the early Schweppes Gold Trophies, winning four of the first five runnings of the competitive handicap hurdle, and the subsequent enquiries that fell little short of iniquitous attacks on his integrity, that Ryan Price is best remembered. The good to come

LEFT: *Hill House and jockey Josh Gifford, 1967*

to win if it could, regardless of which was the more fancied.

The first running of the Schweppes was at Liverpool in 1962 when, in a highly bunched field of forty-two (before safety factors limited numbers), Stan Mellor fell at the second, was badly kicked and sustained severe facial injuries. With prize-money worth the equivalent of about seven normal hurdle races, Ryan entered six horses, and he won with Rosyth, a little chestnut colt owned by Kent dealer Jack Sankey.

The following year, the Schweppes moved to a permanent venue at Newbury. Ryan again ran Rosyth, in spite of considerable training difficulties, which included breaking blood vessels, and disappointing form, which his flat race trainer, Ryan Jarvis, had also experienced in earlier years. He saddled the favourite, Catapult II, as well. In a very fast race, this horse faded two out for Fred Winter, while Josh Gifford bided his time on Rosyth, came through perfectly and beat two subsequent Champion Hurdlers, Salmon Spray and Magic Court.

Ryan Price was called before the Stewards to explain Rosyth's 'abnormal improvement', an inquiry that was then forwarded to London to the National Hunt Committee (which merged with the Jockey Club in 1966). Ryan Price attended the inquiry with a clear conscience and an unswerving belief that the Stewards would accept his explanation – that Rosyth was a 'spring horse' (i.e. one who performs best in the spring) who had been beset by training problems – because it was true. His vet corroborated the veterinary difficulties and told the Stewards the advice he had given the trainer. Incredibly, the Stewards took account of the fact that Ryan led Rosyth out of the paddock, but, as he said in his defence, he couldn't lead both his runners.

At length, the Stewards declared that they were 'unable to find a reason for the reversal of form' of the horse and announced that Captain Price would have his licence withdrawn. At first this appeared to be an open-ended ruling, inviting Press comment that this was worse than a jail term, when at least the length of sentence was known. It then was

out of it as far as racing was concerned was twofold: subsequently, trainers or jockeys called before the Stewards were allowed legal representation, and it was established that certain drugs could be carried naturally in a horse, resulting in acceptable threshold levels being agreed upon.

But this is jumping the gun. Until big sponsored races came into being from the late 1950s, prize-money was low and earnings were often supplemented through betting. For many people, betting still is the perfectly legitimate raison d'être of racing. One thing about Ryan Price was that, even if, or when, he laid out a horse for a particular race, and had advised its owners to bet, he always ran every horse on its merits. Therefore, if he had two or more runners in a race, each was out

ABOVE: *Rosyth (right), ridden by Josh Gifford, crashes through a flight at Newbury, 1964*

clarified that the suspension was until the end of the season; he was also declared a disqualified person, the ultimate racing disgrace, meaning that he could not attend race meetings. It was a devastating sentence, cruelly robbing him of his livelihood. Josh Gifford's licence to ride was withdrawn for six weeks, until 31 March, depriving him of his earnings. All the horses had to leave. The lads, many of whom had sometimes been on the sharp end of the guv'nor's tongue, nevertheless said they wanted to remain, without pay. They were persuaded to accompany their charges as they were dispersed. Within hours, the once thriving stables at Findon resembled a ghost town. In 1965, with a different trainer and three previous unplaced runs, Rosyth finished second in the race. Extraordinarily, when the Stewards returned Captain Price's licence, it was on condition that he trained neither Rosyth nor the horses belonging to four named owners, understood to be betting men.

In 1966, Ryan Price won the Schweppes again, with the maiden Le Vermontois, and this time, thankfully, there were no repercussions. But with Hill House in 1967, it made that awful period with Rosyth almost pale into insignificance. Ryan Price acquired Hill House by chance, when he went to see a hunter in Gloucestershire. The hunter duly became the best of his life. He had had such fun jumping over the farm trying it out with another horse that he enquired about that one, too. The 'other' horse was Hill House, and in return for training him, the owner, Len Coville, gave Ryan Price a half share.

Hill House was always temperamental: he had been for his flat race trainer, Bernard Van Cutsem, and he remained so in later life. When in the mood, he was a lovely ride with plenty of substance and 'feel'; I once cantered him in West Wales, prior to a point-to-point run. Ryan set out to solve the puzzle, which included stabling him in a quieter yard and allowing him to do more or less whatever he liked on the gallops.

Josh said, 'Things had to be done just right for the guv'nor, but with Hill House he always allowed him to have his own way. If he didn't want to go, he didn't force him; the guv'nor was amazing with him. . . . He was a real horseman, very fair and soft at heart; there was nothing he wouldn't do for you if he liked you.'

ABOVE: *Rosyth, ridden by B. Hicks, leads the field at Newbury in 1965*

Of the Schweppes, Josh said, 'It was a lucky race; you do get lucky races', and added emphatically, 'Ryan never cheated.'

Hill House won his first two hurdle races for Ryan, but in the Mackeson Hurdle at Cheltenham he was badly interfered with and nearly came down. This experience put him off, and he was sent back to Gloucestershire for a couple of months' hunting to sweeten him up.

Josh was convinced he would have won the Mackeson Hurdle, but having not done so, and without a run since, he was nicely weighted for the Schweppes on 10st 10lb. But when he first reappeared after his break, Hill House planted himself at the start and refused to race. Next time, only a week before the Schweppes, Len Coville led him in at the start and, a bit ring-rusty after three months off, the horse finished fourth. That brought him on, and a mid-week gallop had Ryan satisfied that he was spot on for the Schweppes, something the papers were already murmuring about. Sadly, when Hill House stormed

clear to win the Schweppes by a wide margin, there was booing from the crowds. Almost inevitably, Ryan was called before the Stewards to explain the improvement in the week since the horse's last run. They told him they considered the improvement 'abnormal' and referred the case to the National Hunt Committee. If found guilty, Ryan Price was likely to be warned off for good. He would need more than a clear conscience on his side this time.

But a much greater shock was in store. A week before the scheduled London hearing, news came that the routine dope sample taken from Hill House at Newbury had tested positive. The sample showed up the steroid cortisol, a 'non-normal nutrient'. This news, apart from coming as a genuine shock to Ryan, made many people who had written to support him begin to have doubts. It was a case in which the scientific experts disagreed in the extreme, and it was thanks in no small measure to one of Captain Price's owners, Lady Weir (two years later to win the Gold Cup with What A Myth), that the truth was finally unravelled. She called in a cancer scientist, Dr G.F. Marrian, at her own expense, to investigate the case. Hill House, it transpired, manufactured so much adrenaline in the excitement of racing (or even travelling, as his subsequent move to the Equine Research Station at Newmarket was to prove) that cortisol was found in his blood.

Dr Marrian wrote: 'The facts, to the best of my knowledge, are as follows. In man, and in many other animals, cortisone, cortisol and a number of closely related compounds are normally secreted by the adrenal glands. These compounds, and some of their metabolic products, appear in the urine, and under

ABOVE: *Jockey Josh Gifford with his fiancée Althea Roger Smith out hunting in 1968*

conditions of stress the amounts of these compounds in the urine are increased.

'While it is possible that cortisone and cortisol may not have been identified in horse urine, it is highly probable that they are normally present. Certainly a number of closely related compounds have been found normally in horse urine.'

This statement was in sharp contrast to that issued by the

Stewards' Advisory Committee.

'The urine sample contained cortisol (Hydro-cortisone).

Cortisol was administered to the horse prior to the race, in a dose sufficient to improve racing performance.

Cortisol is not a normal nutrient.'

After nearly six months, during which Hill House underwent many tests, Ryan Price and all those involved with him, were exonerated completely, 'without a stain on their characters'. And that is how Ryan Price should be remembered. He died in 1987, on his seventy-fifth birthday.

It was only three years after the Hill House case that Ryan Price decided to give up National Hunt training and concentrate on the Flat. He had trained staying flat race winners for years – witness his record in the Cesarewitch – but a new challenge in the form of training two-year-olds seized him. This would offer better prize-money and mostly take place in the warmer summer months, leaving the winter free for hunting.

An astounded Josh Gifford stood chatting with him in his sitting room one day in 1970. 'What are you going to do when you retire?' Ryan asked him.

'Retire?!' the twenty-eight-year-old Josh expostulated. Young, slim, fit, a supreme athlete in the prime of his life, the last thing on his mind was retirement.

But Ryan's surprise announcement brought with it the offer that Josh take over the National Hunt stable, almost lock, stock and barrel, and buy Ryan's part of the house (one end was occupied and not available at the time), the stables and the paddock, with four years to pay. It would mean relinquishing riding. He was not yet thirty, but he had ridden more than 640 winners, had been National Hunt champion jockey four times, had survived innumerable falls – and had been married for a year. Perhaps, one day, he would set up somewhere as a trainer himself. . . . But he wanted one more ride in the Grand National, so Ryan postponed his move for a few months. On 6 April, Josh rode Assad into seventh place in the National, and the next day be became the licensed trainer at Downs House. At

Highland Wedding (on whom Bob won the Eider Chase), Rubstic (whom he 'did' at Toby Balding's before the horse moved to Scotland), Rag Trade (whom he partnered to his first novice chase win) and Corbiere, even though that horse unseated him in a novice chase. He said they all shared the common qualities of being very well balanced with a low head carriage. He was always totally confident Aldaniti would win a Grand National. Even on the morning of the race, Saturday, 4 April 1981, Bob could not contemplate defeat. It was, he said, a formality.

The miraculously recovered Champion and the nursed and nurtured Aldaniti, who had been risked in only one previous race, set out like a partnership inspired. Apart from a mistake at the first fence (where he fell the next year), and a slight error at the second, Aldaniti learnt so quickly that by the twelfth of the thirty fences he had jumped his way into the lead, and there he stayed, sweeping home from amateur John Thorne (later killed in a point-to-point) and Spartan Missile by four momentous lengths. It was the ultimate fairy-tale ending, as the film, *Champions*, later portrayed, although to some of those involved the film was disappointing. 'They cut out many of the sentimental bits,' Josh recalled.

For every dream win in the National – and there is always a good story attached to it – there are many hard-luck tales. Of course, most jockeys have one, but Josh has genuine claims for 1967, when he was second on Honey End to Foinavon, who had been the only horse to avoid the mêlée at fence 23 at the first attempt (see pp.15–16). Josh admitted it was one of the biggest disappointments, but then added, 'On the other hand, there were about eight jockeys who said they would have won!'

Another disappointment was that he never rode in the Cheltenham Gold Cup, as one year he broke his thigh in a fall, and then, within days of returning, broke it again in a bad car accident, so it was the late Paul Kelleway who was aboard What A Myth when he won. He rates Desert Orchid the best National Hunt horse in his lifetime – 'over two miles or three-and-a-half; he would have won a National standing on his head'. He places

Fred Winter at the top of the all-round National Hunt jockeys' tree, 'and a gentleman with it', Johnny Gilbert, Harry Sprague and Jimmy Uttley as former top hurdling jocks, and, on the current scene, Mick Fitzgerald, 'another gentleman'. Humour is never far away from Josh and others of his riding generation, such as Michael Scudamore, Terry Biddlecombe and David Nicholson. 'There is still fun with today's jockeys, although with night meetings the travelling is harder, but there is always good camaraderie in a dangerous sport; there is no time to get big-headed.'

Josh recalled the luck – and humour – of one particular encounter. As a past winning rider, Josh was invited to the Whitbread dinner for successful jockeys, owners and trainers of the Whitbread Gold Cup. First, he and his brother, Macer, were invited to the suite of trainer Michael Marsh at Claridge's for drinks at 6pm.

'He was a man for whom to have arrived at 6.05 would have been rude,' Josh recalled, adding that he can drink gin and tonics all day, but that champagne always goes straight to his head, especially on an empty stomach. On this occasion, champagne was all that was on offer. At the pre-dinner drinks at the Whitbread headquarters in Chiswell Street, it was more of the same, so it was a fairly light-headed Josh who found himself seated between Lord Plummer, then chairman of the Tote, and veteran owner Jim Joel. 'I'm sure I talked bollocks all evening,' Josh surmised, yet a few years later, and having never met him on any other occasion, Jim Joel sent him half his National Hunt horses on the death of his trainer, Bob Turnell.

There were some very successful times ahead, especially in the period when he had Katabatic, formerly with Andy Turnell, and Deep Sensation, winning races such as the Queen Mother Champion Two Mile Chase. But the horse he names as the best he ever trained is Kybo (a certain generation of readers will know what the initials stand for), owned by the late Isidore Kerman who, when at prep school, used to have the initials written by his mother at the end of her weekly letters to him. Sadly, Kybo was killed at Ascot in 1981.

The Grand National, 1981: Aldaniti and Bob Champion

Isidore Kerman was chairman of Plumpton and Fontwell racecourses, two of the prettiest National Hunt courses (my first memory of racing at Plumpton is on foot while at Pony Club camp there). It was Mr Kerman who was responsible for introducing HRH Prince Charles, the Prince of Wales, to racing. With a keen eye for publicity, he arranged an invitation flat race, the Madhatters, at Plumpton, and his coup was securing Prince Charles to ride. The hurdles were pulled out of the ground after

PREVIOUS PAGE: *Bradbury Star, eventual winner (left), ridden by P. Hide, and Second Schedual, ridden by K. O'Brien, in the Mackeson Gold Cup, Cheltenham, 1994*

BELOW: *Prince Charles is greeted by well-wishers after finishing as runner-up on Long Wharf in the Madhatters Private Sweepstakes at Plumpton, Sussex, 1980*

the last conventional race, and thirteen runners set off. Prince Charles rode Long Wharf, the favourite, trained by Ian Balding; Derek Thompson, the TV racing commentator was on Classified (later to finish third in the Grand National for Nicky Henderson); Althea Gifford was on Glamour Show; and I was on 50–1 shot Linatea, trained by another National Hunt character, Jim Old. Linatea set a true pace and loved leading for most of the way, until first Derek and then the Prince, followed by Althea, swept by to finish in that order. Later, Prince Charles had some chasing rides on Alibar, trained by Nick Gaselee, but unfortunately the horse died.

Without hesitation, Josh names the saddest moment of his life as the day his brother and fellow jockey, Macer, died. Macer was three years younger than Josh and began his race-riding career as an amateur, winning, among other races, the Horse and Hound Champion Hunters' Chase at Stratford. Like Josh,

Macer won a Whitbread on Michael Marsh's Larbawn. Macer developed motor neurone disease and died at the shockingly young age of forty. Every three years, Josh holds a superlative open day, and every penny of it goes towards research into the disease.

It was at the end of the 1997 open day, and after he had been paraded by Bob Champion, that I had the great privilege to take Bradbury Star home to begin his retirement as a hunter. Like Ryan before him, Josh takes care to look after his charges after their careers are over. Originally, Josh turned down the offer to train 'Brad' three times. For one thing, with his yard on a roll, he genuinely had no spare stables, and he was a friend of the horse's then trainer, Tom Kemp. For another, the three-year-old bay by Torus was running in hurdle races 'barely above selling class'.

He had been bought as an unbroken three-year-old for 12,000 guineas at Goffs Sales in Ireland by James Campbell. Eventually, when Tom Kemp moved to Scotland, Josh agreed to take the horse, but did not entertain high hopes for him. Brad had 'eight different jockeys in eight races, claiming boys, amateurs. If we wanted to give a lad a chance in a lowly race, we'd say, "put him on Brad".' Not too much was expected of him, so he was not placed in the higher class races. The result was that the horse grew in confidence. As Ben Wise, who used to train further east along the South Downs, used to say, 'let a horse win a seller and he will grow in stature; put him in a big, high class field and he will be out of his depth and will worry' – wise words.

'So when,' I asked Josh, 'did you start having high hopes for Bradbury Star?'

'I never did,' Josh admitted frankly. 'But he just kept on getting better', he said with a note of surprise still in his voice.

Brad's tally of eighteen victories included two Mackeson Gold Cups, a total of eight wins at Cheltenham, plus the shortest of short head seconds to Barton Bank in the King George VI Chase at Kempton on Boxing Day. He was beaten half a length by future Grand National winner Miinnehoma in the Sun Alliance Chase at Cheltenham, where he was also sixth in the

ABOVE: *Bradbury Star, led by Wayne Hardie, at Kempton, 1994*

Champion Hurdle, and fifth in the Gold Cup, a race for which he had been antepost favourite in the early 1990s before injury prevented him from running. Not bad for a horse 'just above selling class' – and he's a smashing hunter. Admittedly, I'm biased.

He Bought a Little Farm Called Ballydoyle: Vincent O'Brien

'Legend' is not too strong a word to use of the man who once

toyed with the idea of opening a butcher's shop in Buttevant.

His father had died, he was short of money, and the

Second World War meant that there was a farming crisis

in Ireland and a lack of racehorse investment in England.

Luckily, enough owners had seen a flicker of what was

to become undoubted genius to send their horses to

the dedicated young man.

Vincent O'Brien

Vincent O'Brien started modestly in point-to-points as a teenager. He ended his illustrious training career straddling the whole international flat-racing and breeding world like a colossus, with five Derby winners and numerous other Classics under his belt. Yet even then he remained quiet, abstemious, almost demure.

His awe-inspiring, record-breaking and all-too-brief sojourn in National Hunt racing saw a triple Gold Cup winner in

ABOVE: *Vincent O'Brien (left) at his stables, Ballydoyle, Ireland*

Cottage Rake (1948–50), a triple Champion Hurdler in Hatton's Grace (1949–51), another Gold Cup winner, Knock Hard, in 1953, and, incredibly, three consecutive Grand National winners from 1953 to 1955: Early Mist, Royal Tan and Quare Times.

He gave all that up for the lure of the Flat, and the creation of Coolmore Stud. He forged an incredible partnership with Lester Piggott, and his horses included the mighty Nijinsky, the last holder of the Triple Crown of 2000 Guineas, Derby and St Leger, in 1970. Even before his National Hunt career ended, he had trained his first Irish Derby winner in Chamier in 1953. Later in the 1950s, his Ballymoss won the Irish Derby, the English St Leger, the Eclipse Stakes, the King George VI and Queen Elizabeth Diamond Stakes, the Coronation Cup and the Prix de l'Arc de Triomphe. His final Derby winner was Golden Fleece in 1982. El Gran Senor won the Irish Derby in 1984, and Sadler's Wells, now a great sire of offspring including jumpers, won the Irish 2000 Guineas the same year.

Vincent's father was an Irish farmer, Dan O'Brien, who, like so many others, kept and ran a few racehorses as a hobby, strictly for pleasure. Reared in Co. Cork, a stone's throw from the scene of that first steeplechase from Buttevant to Doneraile, young Vincent loved the horses and liked to spend all his spare time (and, one suspects, some of his school-time) among them, mucking out, grooming, riding. By his mid-teens, unofficially, he was gradually, almost inexorably, beginning to take over the training. Then there was a point-to-point mare that quite by chance he discovered to be rather good at home against his father's flat horses, so he decided to put her in a flat race and have a little bet. She duly won.

There were shades of Ryan Price in England and, a few decades later, Martin Pipe. Vincent O'Brien was born in 1917, and first took out a training licence in 1943. Ryan Price was born in 1912, and first trained in 1937. Both men were to give up jumping for the Flat, but both left legendary marks on the winter game.

The farm at Churchtown, Co. Cork, where Vincent grew up, was left to an older half-brother; luckily, that brother allowed Vincent to rent the stable yard and gallops. Vincent was always a dual-purpose trainer and right from the start he had good wins on the Flat as well as jumping, but it was Cottage Rake, a horse he failed to sell because of a supposed wind problem, who really put him on the map. The jockeys who rode out and schooled at Churchtown were among the best of their era: Aubrey 'The Brab' Brabazon, Martin Moloney, Bryan Marshall and one of Vincent's younger brothers, the amateur Phonsie O'Brien.

The late Aubrey Brabazon was one of Ireland's great racing characters, full of stories (a few of which I heard over tea one day), who later trained on the Curragh. As a jockey, he was intelligent and a fine horseman, who became Cottage Rake's regular rider. The lyric often recited then is well remembered today:

'Aubrey's up, the money's down,

The frightened bookies quake,

Come on, me lads, and give a cheer;

Begod, 'tis Cottage Rake.'

Cottage Rake was a bonny little horse, exuding presence. He also possessed class and enough speed, at nine years old, to win the Irish Cesarewitch a few months before his first Gold Cup win; Arkle was that age for his third win. At Cheltenham, Cottage Rake was led over the last by Happy Home, whose rider, Martin Moloney, produced a leap out of his mount that gained them two lengths, but the white-faced 'Rake', wearing owner Frank Vickerman's bright red and yellow colours, slipped into his flat-racing top gear for victory. It was a similar story in the following season's King George on Boxing Day over the shorter and flatter course at Kempton.

In the build-up to the 1949 Gold Cup, both Cottage Rake and Hatton's Grace, due to contest his first Champion Hurdle, suffered colds and runny noses. At nine years old, Hatton's Grace was getting elderly for hurdling, but the horse, considered by all who saw him as uninspiring, duly won. It was borderline whether to let Cottage Rake run, as any touch of 'flu could affect his wind, but as luck would have it, the third day of the Festival dawned with severe frost, and the Gold Cup was run a month later. By that time, Cottage Rake was fully fit, and out-sped Cool Customer from the last.

By 1950, only five runners took on the 'Rake', but one of them was Lord Bicester's unbeaten Finure. Cottage Rake despatched Finure with ten lengths to spare. Lord Bicester also owned

ABOVE: *Early Mist, ridden by Bryan Marshall, at Sandown Park, 1957*

Silver Flame, who was to score ten times on the course below Cleeve Hill – a record that still stands half a century later. Trained by George Beeby, Silver Flame won twenty-six of his forty-four starts, was unbeaten in 1949–50 and won a thrilling Gold Cup in 1951 – another to be run a month late because of frost in March – in which three horses (Silver Flame, Greenogue and Lockerbie) – were in the air together over the last. Silver Flame, ridden that day by Martin Moloney, beat Greenogue by a short head.

In 1950, Vincent bought a little working farm for himself, further up-country near Cashel, in Co. Tipperary. It was called Ballydoyle. It was a typical tract of Irish farmland, criss-crossed by banks, ditches and hedges. Vincent set about making gaps in them so that he could create a gallop. That original picture is

ABOVE: *Cottage Rake, ridden by Aubrey Brabazon, wins the 1949 Cheltenham Gold Cup*

virtually unrecognisable when compared with the huge, modern training complex of today, where Aiden O'Brien (no relation) trains Champion Hurdler Istabraq, though, like Vincent, he mainly concentrates on top-class flat horses.

Not surprisingly, owners became keen for Vincent to train for them after his successes with Cottage Rake. Among the new owners was the Keogh family, who placed both Hatton's Grace and Knock Hard with him. Like Vincent, they enjoyed a bet; although not all their gambles came off, the successes outweighed the losses.

Vincent O'Brien was good with horses. He had a feel for and a love of them. He had that natural 'stockman's eye'. He was also meticulous, down to the tiniest detail, and every instruction was written down, as later students were to find. Steeplechasing is a game of chance, but as little as humanly possible was left to chance by Vincent.

BELOW: *Royal Tan (number 2), ridden by Bryan Marshall, jumps Becher's Brook along with Tudor Line (number 9), ridden by G. Slack, at Aintree in 1954*

What Vincent O'Brien achieved in the Grand National was one of the greatest feats in the history of that race, for he produced the winner in three successive years, with a different horse each time. Every one of them – Early Mist, Royal Tan and Quare Times – had their training problems in the build-up. For each of them, to reach the start was an achievement, to win a fine feat shared between horse, jockey, trainer and owner. This is what steeplechasing is all about.

Royal Tan could so easily have been Vincent's first Grand National winner. He had two attempts, first in 1951, when he made a mistake at the second last in Teal's race, and then in 1952, when he fell at the same fence, both times when in contention. He was off the track for 1953, when Early Mist represented the stable. Only eight years old, Early Mist strolled away with that race under Bryan Marshall from the 1952 Gold Cup winner, Dorothy Paget's Mont Tremblant, humping top weight of 12st 5lb. It was third time lucky for Royal Tan in 1954, after one of the race's epic finishes. Three were together at the penultimate: Vincent O'Brien's second runner, Churchtown, who blundered, Tudor Line and Royal Tan. These two fought every one of those 874 yards up the run-in, but Royal Tan, ridden by Bryan Marshall, just prevailed.

During this period in the 1950s, Bryan Marshall was also one of the riders of an amazing steeplechaser called Crudwell, who won a total of fifty races, thirty-nine of them steeplechases with a Welsh Grand National among them. Owned by Mrs D.M. Cooper and trained by Frank Cundell, he carried many other illustrious riders of the day, including Sir Gordon Richards and Lester Piggott on the Flat, as well as Bob Turnell, Atty Corbett, Dick Francis, Michael Scudamore and Fred Winter.

In 1955, the Vincent O'Brien-trained Quare Times, owned by Mr W. H. Welman, was partnered in the Grand National by Pat Taaffe who, a decade later, was to be associated immortally with Arkle. Both Vincent's previous winners lined up again, as did his Oriental Way, ridden by Fred Winter. For three days it poured with rain, and the ensuing heavy ground was thought to be against Quare Times, but he ploughed through it best of all for an easy victory. The fact that Pat Taaffe won many races over the Aintree fences is testimony to his horsemanship as well as his jockeyship; before his association with Arkle, he had been Ireland's champion jockey several times.

Vincent O'Brien was not quite finished with National Hunt racing, and between 1952 and 1959 he sent out no less than ten winners and two seconds from as many runners in divisions of the Cheltenham Festival's Gloucestershire Hurdle, now known as the Supreme Novices' Hurdle. Vincent O'Brien's successes in steeplechasing would be hard to match in any circumstances. Yet that record was dwarfed by what he achieved on the Flat.

LEFT: *Quare Times and Pat Taaffe scrape through the last fence on their way to victory in the 1955 Grand National*

Fifty Years in Steeplechasing: G.B. 'Toby' Balding

Genial Toby Balding is one of those trainers who seems always to have been there. Although he never kept a large stable – generally having about fifty horses – Toby has nevertheless justifiably earned a reputation for spotting and bringing on future National Hunt jockeys, for involvement with the management of the sport and for welfare.

Morley Street, ridden by Jimmy Frost, wins the Champion Hurdle, Cheltenham, 1991

He has also trained two Grand National winners, two Champion Hurdlers, one Gold Cup winner and the winner of two Breeders' Cup Chases in America. This is no mean feat for a man who says, 'I adore racing, but I don't let it rule my life.'

Of the horses he has trained in a career spanning nearly half a century, Toby unhesitatingly nominates Morley Street as his best. Winner of the 1991 Champion Hurdle, and of America's Breeders' Cup Chase in 1990 and 1991, Morley Street possessed versatility, ability and presence, and was not only the perfect model of a racehorse, but also a great character.

Morley Street was produced as a store by Captain Charles Ratcliffe, well known for providing young horses for the élite end of the market, and for schooling jumpers. Toby took jockey Richard Guest with him to view the horse, and Richard hacked

ABOVE: *Toby Balding at his stables with Cool Ground*

the chestnut around a small field. Morley Street floated over the ground and was a natural athlete. By Deep Run, the outstandingly prolific winner-producing Irish sire, the grandam was Bill Shand Kydd's point-to-point mare, Matchboard, not only one of the best point-to-pointers of her era, in the 1960s, but probably one of the best horses from the distaff side ever to have run between the flags. The only reservation Toby might normally have had was that, at 17 hands high, the horse was bigger than his normal mould, but because Morley Street's conformation was so exceptional, he didn't look big. Toby bought him there and then for owner Michael Jackson.

A good horse wins on most courses and on most grounds, but even the best have their preferences, or their 'lucky' courses. For Desert Orchid it was Kempton Park; recently for Lady Rebecca it was Cheltenham; for Red Rum it was Aintree; and for Morley Street it was over the Mildmay course at Liverpool. He won there in five consecutive years and it was only by a short head that it wasn't six, for on his Liverpool début, Morley Street was beaten the minimum distance in a bumpers. These are National Hunt flat races designed for future chasers to give them racecourse experience without obstacles, and are barred to regular flat horses who would have the edge over National Hunt stores. The 'bumper' may only have four runs in such races, plus the Festival bumpers at Cheltenham and Aintree. After this narrow defeat, Morley Street won the 1989 novices' hurdle at Aintree, and from 1990 to 1993 consecutively won the Martell Aintree hurdle.

After his 1991 Champion Hurdle win over Nomadic Way and Ruling, a trip across the pond beckoned. But, insulting though it may seem, it was only as an afterthought, for the same owner's Forest Sun was due to contest the Sport of Kings Challenge, a bonus novices' race. Since one horse was being taken anyway, they figured they might as well take two. It was an early autumn event, and so Morley Street was given some runs on the Flat in preparation, an experience that showed his connections he could also have had a successful career on the level. From six runs, he beat a St Leger winner and was a short

ABOVE: *Morley Street leaps a flight during the Champion Hurdle, Cheltenham, 1991*

head second in the Doncaster Cup. The fences for the Breeders' Cup Chase are soft and offered no difficulties for the hurdler for two years in succession. 'It is an extraordinary meeting,' said Toby, 'and epitomises what racing should be for the English owner, as owners are very well looked after over there. I think the horse would have won a third year, but the owner preferred to have his friends around him when he had a runner.'

Morley Street's chasing career was all too brief. Toby remembers being bitterly disappointed when he was beaten for the first one, but the horse that did so, in receipt of seven pounds, was none other than Remittance Man, who went on to win the Arkle Trophy Chase at Cheltenham that year, and the Queen Mother Champion Two Mile Chase at the Festival in 1992 for trainer Nicky Henderson. Morley Street became a 'bleeder' (broke blood vessels), and the lovely horse fell out of love with racing.

In retirement he went to Jeff Peate in East Sussex, also acting as trainer's hack in Newmarket for Ed Dunlop, whose assistant was Jeff Peate's son, Ed.

There is a romantic story attached to Toby Balding's Champion Hurdler of two years earlier, Beech Road. The four-year-old arrived as part of the package with pupil assistant trainer Jonathan Geake, whose father, Tony Geake, owned the horse. He was beautifully bred for National Hunt racing, being by Nearly A Hand, out of a sister of the late John Tilling's Duke of York. But when he arrived at Toby's, the horse was a lunatic. He had been broken in, run and won in the space of seven weeks, and it was too much for him. At Fyfield, his exuberance was channelled in the right direction which, coupled with his extravagant jumping, soon produced collective gasps. During that first season he made rapid progress from the bottom of the handicap.

He gave jockey Richard Guest – 'a most underrated jockey,' said Toby – his first win at Cheltenham. His win in the

ABOVE: *Eventual winner Little Polveir, ridden by Jimmy Frost, during the 1989 Grand National*

the twelve-year-old joined Toby from John Edwards' Shropshire yard, a Scottish National already under his belt; he had unseated in the previous year's National when going well. He had two good runs for his new owner without once being hit with a stick and was clearly enjoying himself. He was a spring horse, and before the big race he was full of fire and worked brilliantly.

Jimmy Frost had the ride for the National and it was a case of déjà vu. He was always travelling well and, barring accidents, he simply wasn't going to be beaten. He defeated West Tip, National winner of 1986, and The Thinker, Cheltenham Gold Cup winner of 1987, by seven lengths and half a length at 30–1.

'He was a little star,' Toby recalled fondly. 'Little P', as he was known, died in 1999. He jumped out of his field to join the Puckeridge hounds who were hunting nearby, spent all afternoon with them, came home, contracted colic and died.

During the early 1990s, Toby spent a two-year spell away from Fyfield training at the purpose-built venture, Whitcombe, near Dorchester in Dorset, for Peter Bolton. He loved it there, but found 'virtually every racecourse was an extra 100 miles away.' Peter Bolton was a friend as well as one of Toby's owners. For him, the building of Whitcombe was a cherished dream. 'P.B.' tried hard to persuade Toby to move there to train. Eventually, when Toby's business project, BTRB (British Thoroughbred Racing and Breeding Club, a pioneer of racing clubs), was in financial trouble, he gave it deep thought. He was returning home to Fyfield on a murky November evening after a middling, run-of-the-mill meeting at Towcester when a business partner, Trevor Bishop, pointed out, 'If you were going to Whitcombe now, you wouldn't be half-way back.' Lifestyle was, and is, important for Toby. But Peter Bolton's proposition was generous, with a big salary as well as a financial package. In the end, Toby accepted.

Part of the Whitcombe establishment was a chestnut horse called Cool Ground. 'Cool Ground was Whitcombe,' asserted Toby. Toby had been responsible for finding Cool Ground for Peter, and, as a 'seriously good' handicapper, was certain he would make a National horse. He had run well for Whitcombe's first incumbent, Richard Mitchell, who trained there from the original old buildings before the new luxury complex was built half a mile away. Toby began preparing him when he moved to the tranquil Dorset valley, in the middle of Thomas Hardy country, in 1991. Peter Bolton asked Toby to consider entering him for the Cheltenham Gold Cup as a warm-up race for the National, in which he was set to carry 10st 10lb. Toby agreed, believing the horse would be likely to finish about fourth in the Gold Cup and that it would do him no harm as a prep race, especially as the ground was getting soft enough to suit him. So Cool Ground took his chance. 'It was one of the bravest runs, and owed a lot to the forceful riding of Adrian Maguire,' recalled Toby.

He and Peter Bolton watched the race from the Members'

BELOW: A police escort for Little Polveir and jockey Jimmy Frost after their victory in the 1989 Grand National

Lawn, and the finish produced a tremendous tussle between their horse, The Fellow and Docklands Express. The Fellow was trained in France by François Doumen, and finally won the Gold Cup the following year, after two defeats by the smallest of margins; he won the King George VI Chases of 1991 and 1992, a race which the talented Frenchman has also won with Nupsala (1987), Algan (1994) and First Gold (2000).

As Docklands Express, trained by Kim Bailey, The Fellow and Cool Ground battled for victory, Toby Balding and Peter Bolton thought their horse had finished third. They were walking back to the paddock when television commentator Jonathan Powell asked them, 'What does it feel like to come first in the Gold Cup?'

'Pull the other one,' retorted Toby.

'No, look at the replay.'

They did, and there, on the big screen situated opposite the members' stand just beyond the winning post, they could see that their fellow had got up to beat The Fellow, and Docklands

Express (now a hunter in Wiltshire).

Cool Ground, an 'absolute star', won one more race, the Royal Artillery Gold Cup, and was then retired to Toby. 'Jack' (his stable name) relished his new-found role as schoolmaster, leading Toby's string of two-year-olds out on to the gallops, and also went hunting with the South Dorset Hunt.

Toby's list of conditional or amateur jockeys who have gone on to be top professionals over the years reads like an honours academy: Owen McNally; Bill Palmer, for whom Fred Winter had tremendous admiration, and who had been Ian Balding's

BELOW: *Adrian Maguire on Cool Ground riding to victory in the Cheltenham Gold Cup, 1992*

head lad; Bob Champion, who came as an amateur; most famously, Adrian Maguire and Tony McCoy; Barry Fenton; and currently conditional jockey Finbar Keniry.

Toby was looking for a conditional jockey when Tom O'Mahoney in Co. Cork suggested he come and look at an Irish amateur, one Adrian Maguire, whose first winner had been at Sligo in 1989. Two years later, Adrian rode Omerta to win the Kim Muir at Cheltenham for Martin Pipe, before joining Toby as his amateur. The Kim Muir (now the Kim Muir–Fulke Walwyn) is the amateur riders' race originally named after the Cheltenham-based amateur who was killed in action in the Second World War. It was Adrian who rode Cool Ground to victory in the 1992 Cheltenham Gold Cup. He also won the King George VI Gold Cup on Barton Bank, beating Bradbury

Star by a short head in a rousing finish. The Queen Mother Champion Chase on Viking Flagship was an equally thrilling race. Some of his other big race wins have included the Irish National on Omerta, the John Hughes over the National fences at Aintree, the Hennessy Gold Cup on Sibton Abbey, the Irish Champion Hurdle, the Scottish Grand National and the Whitbread Gold Cup in 1998 on Call It A Day. With a list of wins as impressive as that, the only surprise is that Maguire, thirty years old in 2001 and as popular in the weighing room as with the public, has never been champion, but he went through a spell with more injuries than the average National Hunt jockey can usually expect.

Tony McCoy, by contrast, enjoyed a meteoric rise and remains at the top of the table by dint of unflinching hard work, quest for wins, lack of serious injuries and partnership with Martin Pipe. He first became champion in 1995–6, and has remained there to date. An Ulsterman, Tony McCoy was seen by Toby Balding riding at Wexford.

Toby said of him, 'He was accomplished, rode with style, and when speaking to him, he looked one straight in the eye.'

So Tony McCoy, or 'A.P.' as he is often known, from his initials, moved to England as Toby Balding's conditional jockey. He rode Beech Road for Toby, and Viking Flagship, whom he rates alongside Beech Road, Mr Mulligan and Make A Stand (1997 Cheltenham Gold Cup and Champion Hurdle double) as among his best and most memorable rides. Before long it was clear A.P. was 'outgrowing' Toby's comparatively small yard and the future beckoned elsewhere.

Toby assessed Tony, and his predecessor as champion jockey, Peter Scudamore, as 'products of the modern style, pure jockey-ship.' Peter Scudamore's father, Michael, won the 1959 Grand National on Oxo and rode in the race thirteen consecutive times. Peter never won the race, but was champion jockey a record eight times; his son, Tom, is now a rising amateur.

Toby shares the view of most in rating Fred Winter and his protégé John Francome as 'the complete product'. 'They were both beautiful horsemen as well as very good jockeys, and

ABOVE: *Viking Flagship (right) in the Queen Mother Champion Chase, Cheltenham, 1994*

aesthetically correct – that is, good to watch.' Over hurdles, he named Harry Sprague, and then added, 'And don't forget Lester Piggott!' Lester rode over hurdles in the 1950s to keep in trim during the winter to be ready for the Flat season. In 1954, he won the Triumph Hurdle at the Cheltenham Festival on Prince Charlemagne.

Toby named Arkle as the best steeplechaser ever – 'he totally dominated, he was unbelievable and the handicap rules had to be rewritten to accommodate him' – and L'Escargot and Flyingbolt as two unsung heroes, with Istabraq best of those running at the turn of the twenty-first century.

Finding and producing National Hunt jockeys is not the only role to which Toby has given his time and talent. He is also chairman of the National Hunt branch of the National Trainers' Federation, and puts much effort into the welfare side of racing,

ABOVE: *Adrian Maguire rides Barton Bank to victory in the King George VI Gold Cup, 1993*

too. Toby is a trustee of the National Trainers' Federation Charitable Trust, which helps those leaving the industry to retrain in new fields. It mostly funds lads and lasses, the unsung backroom boys of racing, by paying for specialist courses for them. Inevitably, he has seen many changes over the years, but the biggest by far, he says, is in owners.

When he began training, the owner base in National Hunt racing was made up of the landed gentry and farming fraternity, plus a few sportsmen. Pressures on the trainer were very few, mainly because owners understood the problems inherent to training thoroughbred horses. The horse was already a part of their overall lifestyle, so if their racehorse needed time, or got a 'leg', they understood. Labour was cheap, and the emphasis was very much on sport. Toby still has one owner, Desmond Lockyer, a West Country farmer, who has been with him since

he started, with whom no money has ever changed hands. The training fees are paid for entirely through the provision of hay, tractor services and the like. He is a rare gem these days. Today, the landed gentry have become less and less wealthy and barely make a racecourse presence, says Toby. They have been replaced by city industrialists, for whom money is no problem. But, not having the background in racing, they are far more likely to query items on the monthly bill, and do; not nastily, but they are much more demanding in wanting to know how their money is used, and the facilities on which it is used are also more expensive than they used to be. It all makes more work in the trainer's office. Where the staff bill used to be about 20 per cent of the overheads, it is now 50 per cent, although Toby admits the workforce 'used to be virtually unpaid'. Staff shortages today are not because of low pay, he says.

Toby is aware that those in the 'old guard' are wary of change, himself included, but feels that generally changes are made for good, salient reasons and he has radical ideas for the future. He firmly believes that training should be centralised. 'It's crazy to be training in the twenty-first century in the same old separate yards. Racing should be centralised in one state of the art yard per region.'

He uses his nearest training colleagues as examples. The days can, and do, occur when three separate boxes turn up alongside each other at far away places containing horses trained by him, his brother Ian and Richard Hannon who, like Ian, is a flat race trainer for the Queen. All of them train within a pebble's throw of each other.

'I have fifty horses, Ian has 100 and Richard has 200, all in the area, but in totally separate units for the preparation of the same product. We should share transport and training facilities. We have become blinkered and spoilt, but Peter Savill [the hard-hitting chairman of the British Horseracing Board with a big financial plan] is doing a lot allied to centralisation.

'I have worked in racing all my life, looking for this magic pot of money, but it isn't there. Some trainers are wealthy in their own right and keep on going, but others who have to rely on it for earning a living cannot.

'We are the worst funded racing nation, totally because of the bookmakers. Betting takes the top slice. They used to be the only businessmen in the sport, the rest were gentlemen or employees of rich men, still of the top echelon, very able and extremely wealthy.

'There are too many courses and too many horses. France has many country courses where they will have three races for thoroughbreds, two for trotting and one cross-country – but there is plenty of money, as all betting is through the Parimutuel (Tote).

'We have got to make our game more affordable all round,'

ABOVE: *Toby Balding's yard*

he says. Then, slightly going off at a tangent, he concludes on a defiant note, 'If by some awful chance we were to lose hunting, then I think we will lose point-to-pointing and shooting, followed by fishing. We live in a sanitised society.'

Scottish Stories, Middleham Magic and Jumping's Jonjo: Oliver, Crump and O'Neill

Of the same vintage as Ryan Price, Fulke Walwyn

and Vincent O'Brien were Scotland's Ken Oliver,

and northern England's Neville Crump,

two of National Hunt racing's great characters.

Norman Williamson on Deep Sensation, 1995

Ken Oliver trained many winners, but probably the most famous was a loser, who was three times runner-up in the Grand National. But it is not strictly fair to call Wyndburgh a loser. Wyndburgh was a small, close-coupled dark bay whose dam, Swinnie, cost Rhona Wilkinson £22. Rhona bred Wyndburgh and rode him to both of his point-to-point places herself. It is said that the grandam took Fulke Walwyn on an extended view of Kelso, that pretty little course just north of the border, allegedly bolting round it not once but twice.

Ken Oliver married Rhona in 1958, and took out a trainer's licence in 1960. He was already well established as a farmer, an estate agent and a livestock auctioneer, and not long after he co-founded the Doncaster Bloodstock Sales with Willie Stephenson. Like Rhona, he had been a good point-to-point rider, and he was also a successful amateur under Rules, winning the Scottish Grand National riding Sanvina carrying 12st 2lb in 1952, a record-winning weight for the race. One of Sanvina's descendants, also bred by Rhona Oliver, was Deep Sensation, the lovely dark chestnut who won the Tote Gold Trophy of 1990, the 1993 Queen Mother Champion Two Mile Chase at Cheltenham and the 1995 Mumm Melling Chase at Aintree for trainer Josh Gifford and joint owners Robin Eliot, Brian Stewart-Brown, Tim Villier-Smith and Michael Marchant.

The Second World War curtailed Ken's activities – though by all accounts he and his contemporaries enjoyed quite a bit of fun at the cavalry training school at Weedon in Northamptonshire. Among them were Bryan Marshall, Fulke Walwyn, Joe Dudgeon, the British show-jumping captain, and Gerald Balding, father of Toby and Ian, England's polo captain. At one time Joe kept a horse at Rhona's, in Scotland, so that when he was stationed there he could go hunting, sometimes with no more than a rope around the horse's neck. It was six crucial years out of the young men's riding careers, but they all carved their names indelibly in other spheres.

Wyndburgh came as part of Rhona Wilkinson's wedding trousseau. She had already trained him for two runs in the National, with his initial second place, to Sundew, ridden by Fred Winter, in 1957, and fourth in 1958, when the winner was Mr What from Edward Courage's gallant mare, Tiberetta.

In 1959, running under Ken's permit, he was second again in what proved one of the great Grand National hard-luck stories, for jockey Tim Brookshaw rode much of the way without stirrup irons. It was at Becher's second time round that one iron broke. Kicking the other iron free to balance himself, Tim Brookshaw, that season's champion jockey, headed towards the next, slightly smaller fence, and when he negotiated that safely he simply continued, ranging alongside Michael Scudamore on Oxo. He negotiated the Canal Turn without being loosened in the saddle, but the drop fences proved more difficult for, with Tim being unable to help the horse as much as he would have liked, Wyndburgh pecked each time on landing, losing vital ground. This enabled Oxo to poach a bigger lead, and it was not until negotiating the last that Wyndburgh was able to go after him in earnest. Oxo was tiring, and Wyndburgh was gaining with every stride. He failed by just one-and-a-half lengths to get up, and there is no doubt that, but for being ridden virtually bareback for so far, Wyndburgh would have won. In the 1960 Grand National, Wyndburgh made such a mistake at Becher's that even a jockey like Michael Scudamore was ejected from the saddle. There are many hard-luck stories in the Grand National, but Wyndburgh's in 1959 was amongst the most genuine.

It was a tremendous feat of horsemanship from Tim Brookshaw, who was to break his back in a racing fall and, like Paddy Farrell in a similar fall, was paralysed. The fund set up for these two gallant steeplechase riders went on to become the Injured Jockeys' Fund (IJF). Since then, the IJF has become an integral part of the racing scene, and has raised nearly £5 million, of which only a tiny fraction goes to administration. The rest is spent on grants or practical assistance in many different forms to injured jockeys, be they ailing octogenarians or unexpectedly stricken young conditional jockeys with long-term problems, or their dependants. The fund gives immediate emergency help in the most dire cases, even before one of the five almoners has been to visit.

Her Majesty Queen Elizabeth the Queen Mother is the IJF's patron and the chairman is Lord Oaksey, the racing journalist, who, as John Lawrence, came tantalisingly close to winning the 1963 Grand National on Carrickbeg, only to be beaten in the dying strides by Ayala. The trustees are all racing men with the highest degree of knowledge in the field: Bob McCreery, Brough Scott, Dick Saunders, Sir Edward Cazalet, John Smith,

BELOW: Tim Brookshaw guides Wyndburgh over the last fence, without stirrup irons, to take second place in the 1959 Grand National

Peter Scudamore, Simon Tindall, John Fairley, Simon McNeill and Jack Berry. The IJF Christmas card, painted by a different artist each year, is always eagerly awaited and does much to swell the fund's coffers.

Scotland took home the National spoils in 1960 via the Neville Crump-trained Merryman II, whose early days had been hunting with the Buccleuch with his Scottish owner, Miss Winnie Wallace. He had won both the Liverpool Foxhunters and the Scottish Grand National in 1959, and the year after his National victory he finished runner-up. This was the year, 1961,

when the take-off sides of the great fences had, for the first time, been sloped out, forming an 'apron', making them more inviting and slightly easier to negotiate. Wyndburgh finished sixth behind Nicholas Silver, but in 1962 he ran for the sixth time in the race and, for the third time, he was second, this time to Kilmore, and it marked Wyndburgh's honourable retirement.

Ken Oliver and Neville Crump between them made the Scottish Grand National their own, winning it five times each. Ken's wins came with Pappageno's Cottage (1963), The Spaniard (1970), Young Ash Leaf (1971), Fighting Fit (1979) and Cockle Strand (1982). Held since 1966 at Scotland's premier course at Ayr, which basks in the Gulf Stream, the race was previously run at the now defunct Bogside, although some

BELOW: *Cockle Strand (centre), eventual winner of the 1982 Scottish Grand National*

Scottish point-to-points were staged there for about thirty years afterwards. Ayr, where jumping was introduced in 1950 into a course that was previously all flat racing, is a worthy venue for a race of such prestige.

Ken, a man of many parts, was a keen golfer and a great supporter of the Royal Highland Show at Edinburgh, where he revived not only the equine classes, but the flower section as well. 'Yes, flowers were a great interest for him,' said Rhona. The couple's magnificent garden is a legacy to that.

The farm near Hawick is beside the Teviot River, a tributary of the Tweed, and a big flat haugh, or field, gives them a mile-round gallop, as well as a six-furlong grass gallop, with the Minto hills nearby. During the winter of 2000–1, the wettest on record, Rhona said, 'We always used to say we didn't need an all-weather gallop, but even the hills are bottomless this year, the first time in forty years.'

ABOVE: *Neville Crump*

ABOVE: *Sheila's Cottage is led in after winning the 1948 Grand National*

In June 1999, one of the enduring partnerships of National Hunt racing came to an end with the death of Ken Oliver. A few years before his death, Ken, always a great party man, had had a quadruple heart bypass operation, 'one for Tio Pepe sherry, the others for blood', though by the time I first heard the story on a trip north it had been embellished to 'one for whiskey, one for brandy and one for gin'. Rhona, with typical guts and fortitude, has continued training, as well as managing their National Hunt stud. Now in her early seventies, Rhona still rides out two lots a day, 'though I pick my rides a little bit now'. She and Ken were a great team and it is no surprise to find her continuing in the same tradition. After all, there is still a home-bred full sister to Deep Sensation at stud, producing future steeplechasers.

High up on the beautiful Yorkshire Dales lies historic Middleham Moor, above the ancient, cobbled market town of Middleham, dominated by its medieval castle, once the home of Richard III. Middleham, in the heart of Wensleydale, is the North's answer to Lambourn. Among the stables there, secreted in amongst the little side streets of the town and the surrounding area, are, among others, those of Ferdy Murphy, Micky Hammond, George Moore, Patrick Haslam, Kate Milligan and, perhaps most responsible for Middleham's revival in recent years, the vet turned flat race trainer, Mark Johnston. Today, Ferdy Murphy has also done much to restore the prestige of Middleham with a powerful string, and a reputation for winning races at the Cheltenham Festival. He has seen the down side, too, with the death in an accident at exercise of his outstanding chasing prospect, French Holly.

There is the most wonderful sense of freedom up on Middleham Moor. Training facilities have been brought up to

ABOVE: *The field at the first fence in the 1952 Grand National. The eventual winner, Teal, ridden by A. Thompson, is on the extreme left in spots with the quartered cap*

date and transport for reaching far-flung courses is good, too, as the A1, and its associated network, is only a few miles to the east. Middleham had a racecourse on the High Moor in the mid-1700s when training is known to have taken place. Over the centuries some famous flat winners were sent out by the Peacock family and Sam Hall, among others.

For jumping, the name Neville Crump is synonymous with Middleham. For fifty-two years, Captain Crump sent out a stream of the country's best staying steeplechasers from Warwick House, now part of Mark Johnston's enterprise. A keen hunting man and point-to-point rider, Neville Crump first took out a training licence in 1937, having previously served in the 4th Hussars. During the Second World War, he served with

the Royal Artillery Corps, but he lost no time at the conclusion of hostilities in training the first of his three Grand National winners, the mare Sheila's Cottage, in 1948. The favourite was Silver Flame but, though his total of ten wins at Cheltenham remains a record, he did not burn so brightly at Aintree and fell. Lord Mildmay, the popular amateur, was out of luck again. Having had his reins break on Davy Jones in 1936, when the race lay between him and Reynoldstown, this time he suffered debilitating cramp in his neck, forcing his head down and rendering him little more than an unseeing passenger; even so, Cromwell finished third. There was another hard-luck story in this race, too, when Zahia's jockey, Eddie Reavey, took the wrong course past the water jump on the run-in when he looked likely to catch the leader, First of the Dandies. That infamous run-in brought the leader near to a standstill, leaving Sheila's Cottage to catch him.

At Aintree four years later, in 1952, the year of Mrs Topham's

ABOVE: *Merryman II, ridden by Gerry Scott, wins the 1960 Grand National*

RIGHT: *Jonjo O'Neill*

with Much Obliged in 1957 and again with Hoodwinked in 1963, as well as the Hennessy Gold Cup at Newbury with Springbok in 1962. For sixteen of those years, Gerry Scott was, barring injury, his principle jockey, until his retirement in 1972, when he became a Jockey Club starter. Captain Crump continued training until 1989, when, at the age of seventy-nine, he finally retired.

Stan Mellor rode a few times for Neville Crump, notably on Titus Oates in the King George VI and the Cheltenham Gold Cup. He recalled, 'He was a tremendous character, outgoing, and you could hear him before you could see him. He was intelligent, a leader, and a real ambassador for the North. He got a lot of things done for the benefit of racing.' Neville Crump was

farcical attempt at providing the radio broadcast instead of the BBC, Neville Crump was back in the hallowed enclosure with Teal. As in 1951, there were many fallers, but Teal, who had begun life in the hunting field, was a good jumper. Sadly, he died within a year of a twisted gut.

The year 1960, when Neville Crump sent out his next National winner, Merryman II, ridden by Gerry Scott, was the first time the great race was televised. The former hunter chaser had brought his trainer the second of his five Scottish Grand National wins the year before. Wot No Sun won it in 1949, Arcturus in 1968, Salkeld in 1980 and Canton took home the spoils in 1983. Neville Crump also won the Welsh Grand National at Chepstow with Skyreholme in 1951 and Narvik in 1980. At Cheltenham, he won the 1976 Mackeson Gold Cup with Cancello, and in 1978 he took the Massey Ferguson Gold Cup there with his great servant Even Melody, who won an incredible thirty-three races for the captain. Further forays south netted him the first Whitbread Gold Cup at Sandown

a big man in every sense of the word: large in build, booming in voice, expansive by nature. He painted a broad brush across the huge canvas of steeplechasing.

Jonjo O'Neill was an honorary northerner from the time he left his native Ireland in 1972 until he moved south to Jackdaws Castle, Gloucestershire, in the summer of 2001. Like Fred Winter, Jonjo O'Neill is many steeplechasing fans' idea of the

LEFT: *Jonjo O'Neill weighing in, c.1981*

perfect sporting gentleman. He has plumbed tremendous depths in his career, be it from serious injury – he once nearly had to have his leg amputated – or the dreaded cancer, but he has always bounded back smiling. Jonjo worked his way up the ranks and matured into one of the best horsemen in the sport. Being a jockey was all he ever wanted to do, but he had to prove it to his father, Tom, the hard way, by cycling seven miles from home in Castletownroche to school in Doneraile rather than taking the bus.

Living in that part of Ireland meant Jonjo grew up on the legend of the first-ever steeplechase from Buttevant to Doneraile. He started out riding donkeys, before the Warlow family, mother Sheila and daughters Claire and Mary, helped him along the riding road. 'Their mum lent me a hat, and took me to my first hunter trial, then I was given my first pair of jodhpur boots when Claire had grown out of them. I felt very posh with my hat and boots.' It was Mary, who married Wiltshire farmer Robert Wilson and now hunts with the Tedworth, who drove Jonjo on a lap of honour round Castletownroche after he first won the jockeys' championship. Both she and Jonjo still laugh when they recall what a hairy trip that turned out to be, with the pony taking fright and plunging into a parked lorry – luckily just after they had alighted.

Jonjo's first pony was a two-year-old called Dolly, whom he broke in himself and hunted with the Duhallow, which 'fettled me up in every respect; it was the best training for a kid'. He served his apprenticeship in Ireland, and then joined Gordon Richards at Penrith in Cumbria, where he stayed for five years. Stable jockey Ron Barry was a great help to him and remains a hero.

In his first year of riding freelance, 1977–8, Jonjo found himself, to his own surprise, not only champion jockey, but also a record-holder, with 149 wins. He became the fastest to reach the 100 mark in early February 1978, a record previously held by Fred Winter, who reached that figure in mid-March 1953.

Jonjo named the best horse he ever rode as Sea Pigeon (see p. 53). 'He was so fast,' he said. Also among the great horses he rode were Dawn Run (see pp.196–202). Few would disagree with his nomination of her Gold Cup as the best race he ever rode. His favourite horse of all was Alverton, the chestnut on whom he won the 1979 Gold Cup in a snowstorm, in which Tied Cottage crumpled beside him at the last. Just over two weeks later, Alverton was running a cracking race in the National, jumping those fences superbly until approaching Becher's the second time round, when he simply failed to take off. It is believed that he suffered a heart attack and was already dead on landing. Until then, Alverton had pulled Jonjo enthusiastically into each fence, relishing the challenge, rising to the occasion. For Jonjo, what began as the best ride of his life ended in heart-breaking tragedy.

BELOW: *Alverton (eventual winner) and Tied Cottage take the last jump in the Cheltenham Gold Cup, 1979*

Eight years after that, and only a month after his incredible win on Dawn Run, Jonjo suffered a run-of-the-mill fall in the Scottish Champion Hurdle that resulted in him quitting race-riding. 'I fell off backwards, and I knew straightaway that I had had enough.' And so Jonjo, already the owner of Skelton Wood Farm nestled in the Lake District, embarked upon his training career. That summer, weeks rather than months later, he was diagnosed with cancer.

Jonjo, with his typical grit, pulled through and became a respected northern trainer, culminating in 2001 with a runner good enough for the Cheltenham Gold Cup, Legal Right. And on 1 June, he was given the keys to Jackdaws Castle, the purpose-built training complex in the Cotswolds bought a few months earlier by Ireland's biggest owner, J.P. McManus, for whom Jonjo is a trainer. It is typical of Jonjo that he goes into a new century with another goal to aim for. 'I am really looking forward to it,' he said, that effervescence still in his voice.

Lucky of Lambourn:
Some Leading Lights

Lucky is the word that crops up most frequently in the vocabularies of both Nicky Henderson and Johnny Francome, and it is no coincidence that they both started their careers with Fred Winter in Lambourn.

Osbaldeston and John Francome clear the water jump on their way to win at Stratford, 1975

Lambourn is chasing's answer to Newmarket, though the Berkshire village also houses some top flat trainers, such as Barry Hills. But whereas Newmarket has the expanses of the heath on which to train, the more robust National Hunt horses can gallop up the steep hills of the Berkshire downs, as well as on the level. Both terrains are free-draining, with springy, old, unploughed turf, so it is natural that racing communities have built up over the centuries.

Visitors to the village are greeted with the road sign 'Lambourn Valley of the Racehorse'. I call at the chemist to buy some aqueous cream for sore sides. 'It's for my horse,' I explain, needlessly.

'Of course,' smiles the chemist. 'We sell more of our products for use on horses than humans.'

The houses and many stable yards of Lambourn lie snug along the banks of the River Lam. North-west along the Newbury to Swindon road that bisects the village, a lane loops off to the right, and this arc comprises Upper Lambourn, home to many of steeplechasing's greats, both equine and human, past and present. It includes Uplands, made famous by Fred Winter, and, 'over the wall', Saxon House, the home of his great rival, Fulke Walwyn.

BELOW: *A young Fred Winter: at home in the saddle from an early age*

ABOVE: *The field in the Cheltenham Gold Cup, 1961. The race was won by Saffron Tartan, ridden by Fred Winter*

As I write, it is fourteen years since Fred Winter had the fall down the stairs of his home which left him severely disabled – a cruel irony when one considers the 300 racing falls and some severe injuries from which he recovered to ride again. Fred Winter's name is synonymous with steeplechasing and all that the sport stands for: he was generous, kind and honest, sporting, brave and a tower of strength; he was also a superlative rider and trainer. For many, he is the epitome of the gentleman of National Hunt racing.

He is the man who won or placed in half of his 4,000 rides, galloping more than 10,000 miles and over approximately 120,000 fences. He rode with a 'clock' inside his head, and invariably took the shortest route. He won two Grand Nationals on Sundew (1957) and Kilmore (1962), the memorable French equivalent on the broken-bitted and broken down Mandarin (1962), two Cheltenham Gold Cups on Saffron Tartan (1961) and Mandarin (1962) and three Champion Hurdles (on Clair

Soleil, Fare Time and Eborneezer (see p.101).

It was his incredible strength in the saddle for which Fred Winter is best remembered as a jockey. Stocky and quite short, his strength was likened to that of a boxer; he could shift his weight in the saddle, and his legs would pump, pump, pump as he rode a finish, hardly ever resorting to the whip, for that would have interrupted the rhythm of the hands and heels with which he willed his mount on. Only Tony McCoy is generally regarded as matching him in strength. Fred won the jockeys' championship four times and in the 1952–3 season rode 121 winners, a staggering total for those days and one that was not bettered for twenty-five years.

Kilmore was bought specifically for Fred to ride in the National and, although it took two attempts, in 1962 the partnership brought it off. That was a memorable season for Fred Winter, by then approaching the end of a riding career which had begun in 1947 when he was on leave from the Parachute Regiment. In the 1961–2 season, Fred won races in Ireland, America and France, as well as the Cheltenham Gold Cup on Mandarin and the Grand National on Kilmore.

It is for his incredible feat in the French Grand National at Autueil on Mandarin that he is best remembered. Early in the race, Mandarin's bit broke in two, leaving the horse 'rudderless', and Fred was ill through wasting to make the weight for the ride on another horse. In his stupendous effort to keep to the right course and get up to win, the gutsy horse had broken down. It was one of the most memorable steeplechasing wins of all time.

Within two years Fred Winter and his embryo staff, Richard Pitman included, were virtually camping at Uplands as the

BELOW: *Fred Winter on Mandarin, being led in by the owner, Mme Kilian Hennessy, after victory in the Grand Steeplechase de Paris in Autueil, 1962, the broken bit dangling uselessly*

place was renovated around them and being made ready for training. Jay Trump got the stable off to a dream start. Within a decade there was the magical era of the 'famous five': Pendil, Bula, Lanzarote, Crisp and Killiney, later joined by Midnight Court. All of them had wonderful manners and kind natures, although Pendil 'could nip a bit'; of Killiney, tragically killed at Ascot, Fred said, 'He was so kind, he was just like a great big puppy.'

Richard Pitman rode many good winners and in many memorable races for Fred Winter, so it seems tough that two of the best ended in defeat: Crisp in the 1973 Grand National, and Pendil in the Cheltenham Gold Cup. There was not much of Pendil, but he was a total athlete who floated over the ground. When racing fit, he would start 'goose stepping' and he would also try to bite Richard as he dismounted, unless his rider got in quicker with a Polo mint. Pendil was undoubtedly one of the most talented horses never to win the Gold Cup. Twice he was odds-on favourite, but in 1973 he idled in front from the last fence and was beaten by a short head, breaking his eleven-race sequence of wins. The following year he was brought down. Midnight Court redeemed Fred's luck as a Gold Cup trainer in 1978 (see p.153), and to date Fred Winter remains in second place for the number of Cheltenham Festival winners trained behind the clear leader, Fulke Walwyn.

Fulke Walwyn's training career was awe-inspiring, to say the least, and spanned more than half a century, from 1939 until 1990. He won the Cheltenham Gold Cup four times, with Dorothy Paget's Mont Tremblant in 1952, Mme Hennessy's Mandarin in 1962, Mill House the following year and, ten years after that, The Dikler. He also won the Grand National with Team Spirit in 1964; the Scottish Grand Nationals of 1947 with Rowland Boy and 1964 with Popham Down; and the Champion Hurdle with Anzio in 1962 and again in 1965 with Kirriemuir. He trained the winners of the Hennessy Gold Cup, the Whitbread Gold Cup and the King George VI Chase an incredible six, seven and five times respectively. He also won the

Cathcart Challenge Cup, traditionally the 'get out' for punters at the end of the Cheltenham National Hunt Festival, seven times, and he was champion trainer five times. He trained an incredible forty-four Festival winners, currently still a record, 150 winners for the Queen Mother, and over 2,000 winners spanning his career.

Fulke began as an amateur rider from 1929 to 1936, when he won the Grand National on Reynoldstown while serving as a subaltern with the 9th Lancers. He followed the gentlemanly act of the owner's son, Frank Furlong, who had won on the same horse the previous year, in immediately turning professional, having accepted a monetary gift for winning. There were, and are, those who say Reynoldstown's second win was lucky, because it was the race in which Lord Mildmay's reins broke on the leader, Davy Jones, at the penultimate fence. Fulke, ever the gentleman, did not press his claims too vociferously at the time, not wishing to compound Anthony Mildmay's disappointment, but, talking to me in the 1980s, he confirmed, 'I think we would have won anyway.'

The two horses had been neck and neck ahead of the rest of the field on the last circuit until Reynoldstown lost ten lengths with a bad mistake at Valentine's, which is the fence after the Canal Turn. Steadily he made up the lost ground until, sweeping round the long turn approaching the second last, he was nearly upsides again. 'Then I saw Anthony's reins on the ground and I had to check Reynoldstown or he would have been carried out off the course by Davy Jones.'

Fulke saw both sides of the National coin, for although he trained the 1964 winner Team Spirit, in 1967 his Popham Down, admittedly loose, was primarily responsible for causing the wholesale carnage at the 23rd fence. Two loose horses were leading when they swerved broadside the full width of the fence on the take-off side, causing the runners behind to collapse like a pack of cards. All the runners bar one either fell, were brought down or brought to a standstill, until Foinavon, guided by Johnny Buckingham, now a jockey's valet, popped through a small gap on the wide outside and carried on solo to a 100–1

ABOVE: *Fulke Walwyn on Mandarin*

victory, chased in vain by the remounted Honey End.

The Dikler was not expected to win the 1973 Gold Cup. Pendil was odds-on favourite, as he was to be again, in vain, the following year – part of Fred Winter's run of bad luck in the premier race. The Dikler was a big, strong, hard-pulling bay by the prolific National Hunt sire Vulgan, and had a mind of his own with a wilful streak. He had various bits and nosebands fitted to try to restrain him, and it was no use having a jockey who would fight him. A certain amount of equine psychology came into play, and the professional who brought out the best in him was Irishman Barry Brogan. The Dikler began life in point-to-points; although he won two, he ran out in the other. He was not dissimilar when in training, but it is to Fulke Walwyn's great credit that The Dikler, named after a stream in the Cotswolds, ran in six successive Cheltenham Gold Cups. The first was in 1970 when he fell, and the last in 1976, aged thirteen, when he finished eighth behind Royal Frolic. In between, he was third in L'Escargot's second victory in 1971, third again in 1972 to the mare Glencairaig Lady, having led over the last

BELOW: *Reynoldstown, ridden by Fulke Walwyn, takes Becher's Brook for the second time en route to his eventual win in the 1936 Grand National*

fence, and won in 1973. In 1974, he overtook Captain Christy at the last fence, only to be run out of it on the hill. When Ten Up's rider, Tommy Carberry, wore Anne, Duchess of Westminster's colours to victory in 1975, The Dikler was pulled up.

The 1974 victory of Captain Christy was a memorable come-back race for Bobby Beasley, winner of the 1961 Grand National on Nicholas Silver. Bobby was a descendant of the four famous nineteenth-century Beasley brothers whose Grand National record between them was four wins, six seconds and two thirds. All four – Tommy, Harry (Bobby's grandfather), Willie and Johnny – rode in the race of 1879, in which Tommy placed highest at third on Martha behind the winner, Liberator. Between Nicholas Silver and Captain Christy, Bobby Beasley had been to the depths of hell via the demon drink, but had shown great strength of character in getting himself right again.

Fulke's career is indeed an integral part of any celebration of

The Dikler, ridden by Ron Barry, Cheltenham Gold Cup Winner, 1973

ABOVE: *Trainer Jenny Pitman welcomes Grand National winner Corbiere home in 1983*

the history of steeplechasing, and there was no one more appropriate to take on the Queen Mother's horses after the death of Peter Cazalet, or more fitting to be bestowed with the honour of Commander of the Royal Victorian Order (CVO). Two of the best known horses he trained for Her Majesty were The Argonaut, who won six races, and Special Cargo (see p.95), who became a military race specialist and an outstanding winner of the Whitbread Gold Cup of 1984, in one of the closest finishes imaginable at the end of 3 miles 5 furlongs, the greatest of his twelve wins. Fulke died in 1992, and, appropriately, his name

has been added to the Kim Muir, creating the Fulke Walwyn Kim Muir Amateur Riders' Handicap Chase over 3 miles 1 furlong on the opening day of the Cheltenham Festival.

Also located in Upper Lambourn is Weathercock House, the stables from which Jenny Pitman sent out Burrough Hill Lad (her 'Ferrari') and Garrison Savannah to win the Gold Cups of 1984 and 1991, and Corbiere (her 'Ford Escort') and Royal Athlete to win the Grand Nationals of 1983 and 1995. She was the first woman trainer to achieve either feat. One should note here that women were not granted licences to train until 1966, and only then because the intrepid Florence Nagle, at the age of seventy-two, had taken the Jockey Club to court and won. She was joined by Norah Wilmot and Louie Dingwell, three valiant ladies with admirable First World War records, who had had to train with licences held in their head lads' names.

Kim Bailey also sent out a Grand National winner, Mr Frisk, from Upper Lambourn in 1990, and in 1995, with jockey Norman Williamson, brought off the Gold Cup/Champion Hurdle double with Master Oats and Alderbrook. He now trains from his native Northamptonshire. Another Upper Lambourn trainer, Nick Gaselee was responsible, among other achievements, for training for Prince Charles and for tutoring him in race-riding. Nick had an excellent grounding as assistant trainer to Fulke Walwyn and rode over 100 winners himself as an amateur. In 1992, the year of a General Election, he, too, sent out a Grand National winner, in the big, nearly black horse appropriately named Party Politics. Brothers Simon and Oliver Sherwood both train in Upper Lambourn, both previously having been champion amateur riders. It was Simon who set up a winning sequence with Desert Orchid (see pp.202–7).

Off at a tangent from the Wantage end of Lambourn are the more isolated yards in Mile End, Folly Road and Sheep Drove. Seven Barrows was formerly Peter Walwyn's and now, after some Lambourn musical chairs, is the lovely location for Nicky Henderson. Atop the Sheep Drove is the self-designed home of Johnny Francome.

Johnny Francome, arguably the best National Hunt rider of all, never intended to become a jockey, knew nothing about racing and cared even less. He was far more likely to become an Olympic show-jumper and won a junior gold medal for Britain. It was sitting on donkeys on the beach at Barry Island during annual summer holidays from his Swindon council house home that got Johnny hooked on riding. He progressed to the milk delivery pony around the streets of Swindon, and eventually he pestered his parents into buying him a pony. The purchase price of £50 included a bridle and, for a year, John rode bareback; this is doubtless how he derived his superb seat and balance. Soon it was gymkhanas and show-jumping competitions, and that team gold medal. One can imagine the pride and joy of his father, Norman, late mother, Lilian, and twin sisters, Jill and Norma. His is a family that is still closely knit and one in which the parents instilled high standards in the children from an early age.

At sixteen, it was time for Johnny to find a job and, mainly because it was not too far from home, he joined three other lads as apprentices to one F.T. Winter. The course of John Francome's life changed at that moment. 'I was not remotely interested in racing, had never heard of Fred Winter, and in the evenings I would watch the rugger in preference to racing – and I wasn't even very keen on rugger,' he recalled.

This was the era of Crisp, Bula, Pendil, Sonny Somers, Lanzarote and Soloning. The yard had already trained two Grand National winners, Jay Trump and Anglo in 1965 and 1966, Fred Winter's first two seasons as a trainer. The stable jockeys, Paul Kelleway and Richard Pitman, were good to the young Francome. Inevitably, the lad was soon inextricably engrossed in the steeplechasing game, although a broken wrist on his second ride and a permanent weight problem almost caused him to call it a day before any of us had heard of him.

His first ride was a winning one, on a tiny little mare called Multygrey trained under permit by a farmer called Godfrey Burr near Swindon. He broke his wrist on his next ride, but a headstrong horse called Osbaldeston eventually put him on the winning streak that remained for all fifteen years of his career.

ABOVE: *John Francome*

He spent those years with Fred Winter, 'and never a cross word' – bollockings, yes, but no actual fall-out.

Johnny summed up his career modestly. 'I was always lucky, in the right place at the right time, lucky with relatively few injuries, riding for a stable with wonderful horses, helped a lot by Richard Pitman.

'Yes,' he said with that shake of his dark, curly locks and little grin, so familiar to Channel 4 viewers, flickering across his ever youthful face, 'I have had a really good time, met a lot of nice people, and would certainly do it all again.'

Johnny paused before naming his career highlights. They included a Champion Hurdle on Sea Pigeon for Peter Easterby; two King George VI Chases, in 1982 on Wayward Lad for Michael Dickinson and in 1984 on Burrough Hill Lad for Jenny Pitman; a Schweppes Gold Trophy on Donegal Prince for Paul Kelleway; two Colonial Cups in America on Flatterer; and placing twice on Rough and Tumble in the Grand National. Many of the races were, one gets the impression, just part of his profession. 'But winning the Gold Cup for Fred Winter on Midnight Court was very special. He had had a string of losing

John Francome on Midnight Court wins the Cheltenham Gold Cup in 1978

favourites. I knew I was coming up for a lengthy ban for being involved with bookmaker John Banks, which could have got me the sack, and the horse had really nice owners in George and Olive Jackson. They are genuine supporters for whom winning comes second to the safety of horse and jockey.'

Midnight Court joined Uplands from Ireland, and was soon winning staying hurdle races and then novice chases. Always a kind horse, he came back in from his 1977 summer holiday physically furnished up and more powerful, and began winning at premier courses, so Fred Winter decided to aim for the Gold Cup instead of a big novice final. It was a decision that ultimately was helped by a fall of snow. The third day of the Festival in mid-March had to be abandoned, as the course was covered with a thick white blanket. The Gold Cup was rearranged for a month later. Midnight Court, meanwhile, kept on improving. Although Midnight Court was favourite, Fort Devon, trained by Fulke Walwyn, was well fancied. The race itself was copy-book Francome. Poised in second or third on the rails throughout, he slipped the bay horse up the inside of Fort Devon, who was drifting right on the last bend, and a superb leap at the last put the issue beyond doubt.

Francome also highly rates riding three winners at the Cheltenham Festival of 1981: Sea Pigeon in the Champion Hurdle, Friendly Alliance in the Grand Annual Two Mile Handicap Chase and the stayers' hurdle on the full horse Derring Rose who 'on his day was very good'. He could not recall whether it was the year Sea Pigeon beat Monksfield or Pollardstown (it was the latter), nor did he remember under which banner the stayers' hurdle was then run (it was the Waterford Crystal, now the Bonusprint), but he did remember that it was a day when his father and the footballer Don Shanks had come to the races with him and won themselves 'a few quid'. Family and friends took, and still take, precedence over the 'day job'.

Celebrating was hard for John because of the perennial weight-watching, but he said, 'Half the fun of racing was having a laugh with the lads in the weighing room.' For those who do

not make it into the big time, and therefore never earn much money, it is nevertheless 'a far better way of life' than most of the alternatives.

Johnny, one of the great stylists and horsemen, as well as a superlative jockey with instinctive racecraft skills, does not think much of the present standard of riding, apart from that of a handful of jockeys at the top. 'How a lot of jockeys doing quite well can watch Tony McCoy and then think that how they are riding is good enough beats me.' Never afraid of speaking his mind, Johnny added, 'They don't work hard enough at improving their riding; there are about thirty who should be an awful lot better. It's not that they need brain surgery, they just need to apply themselves better.'

Of a previous generation, Johnny rates Jeff King, now training near Marlborough, Wiltshire, the best and, of the present day, unquestionably Tony McCoy. At the lower end of the league there are, he agrees, a lot of jockeys who simply don't get the opportunities, never find that lucky break. Others fail through not pushing themselves enough. He castigates some large trainers who employ an outside 'big name' to ride in preference to their own up and coming jockeys attached to the yard.

One can look back to the old-fashioned late George Owen who 'produced' three professional champions and one amateur, sticking by them no matter what until they had made their names: Dick Francis, Tim Brookshaw, Stan Mellor and amateur Stephen Davenport. Today, trainers find themselves under pressure from owners to put up a 'big name', yet how does a jockey become a star without first being given the opportunities?

John Francome reserves his biggest bleat for falling standards, and specifies 'scruffy lads with filthy tack on dirty horses'.

'At Fred Winter's, everything was done properly; I hate falling standards more than anything else. I don't think you can do justice to looking after more than three horses, but now there are sometimes six or seven per lad.' This, he says, is because 'too many people have got horses who shouldn't be able to afford them; it costs too much. They complain about the level of prize-money, well, don't race then. There are too many bad horses.

'On the other hand, if someone is daft enough to pay £250,000 for a jumper [almost certainly a gelding], well, it's a free world. Training fees should reflect a lad's wages; for looking after three, their money should go up significantly. But there are also some lads so moderate that they should pay for the privilege of riding out. Training fees need to go up so there can be more good lads paid better, who do the job properly. You get what you pay for.'

Johnny names his own lowest spell as the year in which he shared the jockeys' title with Peter Scudamore (1981–2). 'Fred's horses just weren't running well, and when Scu went twenty ahead of me it really geed me up competitively. It was one of those frustrating periods that many jockeys get most of the time.' Scu then broke a leg, bringing a premature end to his season, and Francome, memorably, called it a day once he had equalled Scu's tally, thus sportingly sharing the title.

It was one of seven riding championships for Johnny, one of the great all-round sportsmen. He still plays football every week for the jockeys' team, 'a really good lot of chums, played in the right spirit', and is an able golf and tennis player. He sometimes rides a pony and he still schools occasionally for Nicky Henderson.

Johnny Francome tried his hand at training, after increasing weight caused him to quit the racing saddle in 1985, but he has found his niche as a television racing presenter. He also owns a number of businesses, mostly fish and chip shops and caravan sites, and is a successful novelist. This is where the discipline still comes in. Every morning, even if the sun shines and friends are beckoning for a game of tennis, he spends time in the study of his beautiful and tastefully built home researching and writing his latest racing novel, producing one every year.

Before I leave, I ascertain that I can ring him to check any details from my notebook. 'Of course,' comes the answer, followed by a chuckle. 'It's easier for me, I can make up my writing!'

Outside, his father, who lives in a cottage within the grounds, tends the garden, including the meticulous topiary. One of his sisters teaches in the village, and the other is an interior decorator not far away at Bicester. Both have successful children. As Johnny says, 'Parents are everything. I was so lucky.'

One of the finest National Hunt training feats of the 1980s was that of Nicky Henderson with See You Then, for the horse possessed legs of such delicate porcelain that it was a wonder he won one Champion Hurdle, let alone three. Nicknamed See You When? by the Press, See You Then could only ever be expected to stand one prep race before the Champion Hurdle, but his ability was such that he carried all before him on each occasion. His hurdling was scintillating, flamboyant, fast and accurate. He was also nearly savage in the stable but, being a horse of the highest calibre, he was, of course, forgiven an awful lot. Even fifteen years on, Nicky remembers him with love and affection.

Bred of the highest class, by a Derby winner Royal Palace out of a Tudor Melody mare, it was over hurdles, and not in the Derby, that he made his name, winning the Champion Hurdle successively from 1985 to 1987. Before he could achieve that, his astute trainer had not only to keep him sound, but also to dissuade his owners from sending him to Italy to race, bringing Nicky's skills of tact, diplomacy and gentle persuasion into full play. John Francome, due to ride him in his first Champion Hurdle, a 16–1 shot, was injured in the previous race, allowing Steve Smith-Eccles a dream spare ride; he then kept the ride after John retired.

Seven Barrows, where Nicky Henderson trains, is a constant hive of activity. 'I can give you twenty minutes,' he tells me, then the phone rings. He and his long-standing secretary, Rowie, she of the dalmations, share the calls; each one is noted meticulously in that day's diary. To each caller, Nicky speaks with enthusiasm and courtesy; each is given time, no matter how short of that commodity he is at that moment. A huge wall board containing the names of more than 100 horses, in alphabetical order, with

ABOVE: *See You Then, ridden by Steve Smith-Eccles, leads Gaye Brief at the last in the Champion Hurdle, Cheltenham, 1986*

the recent handicap ratings beside each name, is his useful aide-mémoire, along with the day's copy of the Racing Post. He tells an owner, 'Well, he's well in at the weights', or 'He's high in the handicap, I think we'll put up our amateur and take seven pounds off his back.' Or the conversation is about a youngster. One imagines the owner on the other end can see as well as feel Nicky's beam as he declares, 'It's time to name him and to register colours. He can run in a month. He's done everything perfectly: he's tucked in behind, he's gone between two, and he's quickened and gone ahead with his ears pricked when asked. And he's schooled really well.' One gathers that this was a horse who arrived with 'an attitude problem', now evidently resolved. I can't wait to hear what he is named, so that I can follow his future. All I know is that he is by a fashionable sire.

Feeling involved in the racing game is the big attraction. For

most, that involvement is betting. Many a Saturday armchair viewer gets to know the horses and those caring for them via the television. Others prefer the atmosphere on course, and still more know an owner or someone with 'a leg in a horse', thanks to the increasing number of syndicates and clubs, which enable the 'man in the street' to become a part of the action.

For me, it was taking part, as I was lucky enough to become one of the first women to ride in a steeplechase, closely following the change of law on 29 December 1975. The late Sue Horton, née Aston, was the first to be granted a licence, and had her first ride on 18 February. The first woman to ride under National Hunt Rules was Muriel Naughton at Ayr on 30 January 1976. The first to win, just a week later, was none other than Nicky Henderson's future wife, Diana Thorne, beating her own father, John, in a photo finish in a hunter chase at Stratford on 7 February. Extraordinarily, the second to win was Diana's twin sister, Jane, in a hunter chase at Warwick.

In the same month, on a typically dank steeplechasing day, I rode Log in a hunter chase at Lingfield Park and it was good just to get round. The highlight was Fred Winter's parting words of advice, 'Keep cool, use your head, and enjoy yourself afterwards'. Afterwards, having seen me nearly fall off at the open ditch, he asked, those lovely eyes twinkling and his smile creasing up, 'What were you whispering into your horse's ears?'

A good many male jockeys and trainers were against women riding under National Hunt Rules, yet on the day of a race, the top ones were invariably supportive. Bob Champion is one I can think of who was publicly 'agin', but going out with him for a race at Fontwell one hot August day, he could not have been kinder. When it comes to it, in steeplechasing, there is a feeling of camaraderie among participants.

Cantering down to the start of a selling hurdle at Stratford, one of the professional riders called out, 'You'll keep on the wide outside, dear, won't you?'

Riding an outsider, formerly blinkered, who had become sickened of the game, I jumped him out of the gate and set off in front, intending to allow him to enjoy himself, which clearly he did, bowling along unrestricted. As we rounded the home turn heading for the last flight, I could hear the pounding hooves behind and fully expected to be 'swallowed up' in a few strides, but it didn't happen, and my lovely partner stormed home to victory. Twenty-four hours later, my pregnancy was confirmed, so I reckon my son has his place in steeplechasing history, too.

But I digress. That horse was from my mother's three-horse permit and point-to-pointing yard. Nicky Henderson rode Log for us in a hunter chase before the law changed allowing women to ride. He is now in charge of one of the biggest and most successful National Hunt yards. He, too, began as a 'genuine amateur', and what fun it was, he recalled, in the era which saw the likes of Jim Wilson, George Sloan and Peter Greenall (now Lord Daresbury).

'I was very lucky [that word again] to be with Fred Winter,' Nicky said. He was Fred's assistant from 1974 to 1978 when one of the best horses he rode was the prolific winning hunter chaser,

Rolls Rambler, on whom he won the prestigious Horse and Hound Champion Hunters' Chase at Stratford, which brought down the curtain on the 1977–8 season and on Nicky's riding career. Earlier that season he had partnered Spartan Missile to victory, in a hunter chase at Towcester, and recalled, 'I knew then that he was exceptional, but Fred needed me for another horse next time and my future father-in-law, John Thorne, took over the ride himself.'

John Thorne's riding was in the best tradition of steeplechasing spirit. An amateur in his fifties, he ultimately drove Spartan Missile into second place behind Aldaniti in the 1981 Grand National. Aldaniti and Bob Champion's achievement was the ultimate fairy-tale, but the gallant runner-up could, surely, go one better the next year. Tragically, before that could be attempted, John Thorne was killed riding a home-bred novice horse in a local point-to-point. History was made in 1982 when another amateur, forty-eight-year-old Dick Saunders, a farmer and Master of the Pytchley Hunt, became the oldest rider ever to win the great race, riding Grittar.

Nicky Henderson married Diana Thorne less than a month after he gave up riding and began training. He, too, came within a stone's throw of winning the Grand National in his first season as a trainer, with Zongalero, runner-up to Rubstic in 1979. Since then, he has become something of a Cheltenham specialist, saying, 'We have been lucky to go to the Festival with some strong ammunition.'

It was entirely appropriate that on the death of Fulke Walwyn many of the Queen Mother's horses were transferred to Nicky. His greatest remaining ambition is to train a Festival winner for the centenarian.

Nicky Henderson remembers his days with Fred Winter with great nostalgia. Then he says, 'And to think, I thought how nice it would be to be my own boss and in charge.' He waves a hand airily around the office, those round, bright eyes popping as ever, laughing at the unspoken thought that clearly the job is in charge of him. 'Not that I would want it any other way,' he adds, adrenaline pumping.

The phone rings again and he responds with the same charm, the effervescent enthusiasm. 'There's one in the race was second in a bumper last time, that'll be favourite,' he tells the owner. 'That's the one we have to beat. But your boy is in excellent shape, I really think he should be able to win. There's just that one horse might beat him. Still, I think yours is probably good enough. No, I'm so sorry, I just can't get to Ludlow myself today.' With Nicky, there are no promises, no 'put your shirt on', no bluffing, just, 'I think we should win, but there is one possible danger.'

The next morning, I look in the paper. The Henderson horse had duly beaten the favourite. Outside, on the lawn in front of

BELOW: *Sea Pigeon (right), ridden by John Francome, winning the Champion Hurdle, Cheltenham, 1981*

the lovely Seven Barrows house, workmen are preparing for Nicky's fiftieth birthday bash at the weekend. It is to take place in the evening of Cheltenham's Tripleprint meeting in December 2000, and, Marlborough, Dusk Duel and Geos all enhance their Festival prospects by winning for the stable – what a birthday present. They were ridden by Mick Fitzgerald, a gentleman of a jockey who had to struggle to make his mark when owners wanted a proven name, but who now is so in demand that he simply cannot ride them all. Nicky's feelings on jockeys and the right way to treat them, one surmises, are similar to those of John Francome.

Both the house and the office look out on to the large, square, black and white stable yard. 'I wouldn't want to be far away from the horses,' says Nicky who, bar two essential, stamina-restoring annual holidays, seldom is.

The Pipe Dream: A Quest for Knowledge, A Thirst for Success

One forgets that the intensity of Martin Pipe is not new, for there was a young man at roughly the same time who was just as intense, equally successful (for a few seasons) and whose motto of 'learn, learn, learn' carried him towards his goal of continual improvement.

T hat young man was Yorkshireman Michael Dickinson, a tall, lanky, former champion amateur, who swept all before him when he took over the reins of his parents' establishment in the early 1980s. As a trio, they made the ideal team, with Tony Dickinson buying the horses, his wife, Monica, responsible for the feeding and Michael training and placing the horses. It was not a question of having everything handed to him on a plate, silver-lined. Like many a son, he was determined to try out new methods, rather than simply follow in his father's footsteps.

ABOVE: *Michael Dickinson's famous five (left to right): Bregawn, Captain John, Wayward Lad, Silver Buck and Ashley House*

Unlike Martin Pipe, Michael Dickinson grew up in the world of hunting and point-to-pointing, which progressed into National Hunt racing. He was champion amateur rider in 1969–70, and then rode as a professional until 1979, winning five races at the National Hunt Festival at Cheltenham, as well as several prestigious hurdle races and steeplechases.

Even then, he was looking ahead to a future as a trainer and twice he wrote to Vincent O'Brien in Ireland asking if he could spend his summer break as a temporary pupil with him. Both attempts drew negative replies, so for the third try, Michael drove all the way from Yorkshire to Epsom to ask the maestro in person. Michael's philosophy was simple: if he wanted to be the best, he must learn from the best. He literally followed Vincent O'Brien's every step with notebook and pen in hand that summer. What he learnt in particular was the enormous attention paid to detail. It is no surprise to find Michael's entry under 'recreation' in the Turf directory of that period as 'work'.

Michael was rewarded in his first season of training in 1980 with a winning strike rate of almost 50 per cent, and in his second by becoming champion trainer. When, on Boxing Day, 1982, he sent out a total of twelve winners at meetings across the length and breadth of Britain, one might have thought he had reached an all-time pinnacle, but he was looking forward to the Gold Cup and dreaming a seemingly impossible dream.

Two months later, beleaguered by set-backs, he feared he would have no Gold Cup runners at all. The problems were resolved, and in March, with 100 winners for the season already under his belt, Michael Dickinson had his finest training achievement of all: his horses filled the first five places in the Cheltenham Gold Cup, paling the previous year's superb one–two with Silver Buck and Bregawn. Those two stable stalwarts were in the line-up again for 1983, along with Captain John, King George VI winner Wayward Lad and Ashley House, and the owners of all five were happy to be taking each other on.

Combs Ditch, trained by David Elsworth, was seriously backed, and Fred Winter had two runners, Fifty Dollars More and Brown Chamberlin, but it was the tiny, almost scrawny Bregawn who started favourite, in spite of his increasing propensity to refuse to start. Bregawn's lad safely led him in at the start and, after a few fences, his jockey Graham Bradley, deciding the pace wasn't fast enough, slipped into the lead, where he remained. Four fences from home he was well clear, but a mistake at the second last saw him challenged strongly by his stable companions. Graham Bradley, showing marvellous judgement, aided his brave companion to hang on all the way to the winning post, five lengths clear of Captain John. Wayward Lad was third, Silver Buck fourth and Ashley House fifth.

Michael Dickinson, aware that it was an achievement simply to get one horse to the line-up, let alone win it, had lost a stone in weight through worry in the month before the race, especially once bets started being placed on his horses filling the first five

places. Touchingly, Edward Gillespie, managing director of Cheltenham Racecourse, allowed all five into the unsaddling enclosure.

Within a year, Michael Dickinson had relinquished the all-conquering family yard to take up the role as private flat-racing trainer to Robert Sangster at Manton in Wiltshire. The drive was the same, as was the commitment and the work, work, work ethos, but for some reason or other it didn't gel. In 1987, Michael moved again, this time to Maryland, USA, along with head lad Brian Powell. He trained forty horses for the Flat with considerable success, including the Breeders' Cup Mile and a string of other graded races. In 1998, he moved to Tapeta Farm on 200 acres at the north end of Chesapeake Bay. There his

RIGHT: *Michael Dickinson*

LEFT: *Bregawn, ridden by Graham Bradley, in the Cheltenham Gold Cup, 1983*

training facilities include five turf tracks, one all-weather, eight horse exercisers, a wooded trail and an irrigation pond. Set between New York and Washington DC, it is within easy reach of eleven major racetracks.

Michael's enthusiasm was evident in 2001. 'It is considered to be the best training facility in the USA, not by an inch, or a yard, but by a mile,' he said. It would seem that Michael feels at home in Maryland, and more relaxed. He cites Belmont Park, New York, as his favourite racecourse, and it is good to see that he now lists fox-hunting instead of work under recreations in the current Turf directory. Wayward Lad came to him and hunted for eight years, and now lives in honourable retirement there.

If ultimately Michael's National Hunt training career in England proved short-lived, there is another equally meteoric and successful trainer who remains very much at the top of the statistical tree, who had already trained his first big race winner before Michael Dickinson began training, but who was to have to wait a few more years before truly entering the big time.

From bookmaker's son, bookmaker's runner, bookmaker, to trainer, taking bookmakers' money: it was an unorthodox entry into training, but with it came Martin Pipe's unquenchable thirst to learn more, and a refreshing honesty about his own previous limited knowledge. He has transformed traditional training and broken just about every record. If a horse comes to him with a bad reputation, be it for jumping, temperament, injury or loss of form, Martin Pipe never simply accepts it. He sets about exploring the reasons, and then resolving the problems.

The highest profile case was Carvill's Hill, formerly expected to bring the Cheltenham Gold Cup back to the Co. Dublin stables of Jim Dreaper. He had ended his Irish career with a heavy fall resulting in pelvic injuries. When he arrived at Pipe's six months later, he was despatched to Bristol University, where almost every inch of him was scanned, and a dropped pelvis resulting in muscle wastage in his hindquarter was diagnosed. He was in pain and aggressive, but eventually the lass entrusted to care for him won him round. Mary Bromiley, horse physiologist, worked on the injury, followed in due course by remedial

Rolling Ball wins the Sun Alliance Chase, Cheltenham, 1995

them, it is hard to conceive that the fittest National Hunt horses of all stem from this one field in Somerset. The answer has to lie in the training.

Attention was drawn to Martin Pipe through the sheer scale of numbers. In the early days, he did not have the patient, wealthy owners willing to wait for their horse to mature and then, with luck, be able to keep on running. As the winners began to roll in, he was able to improve facilities: all-weather gallops, horse-walkers, weighing machines, equine swimming pool, laboratories. . . . He suffered the ignominy of being 'investigated' by the Cook Report on television, supposedly for 'cruelty' due to the high wastage factor. Pipe came out creditably, but one could forgive him for being less trusting in

future. He was not at the 'posh' end of racing. He developed his own training methods. The 'old school tie tradition, it's just not done, old boy', did not apply to him, especially in buying horses out of selling or claiming races. The rules stated that he could do it, so he did. In particular, he started buying horses out of French races, with great success.

Martin Pipe is a man who is who he is, no pretensions, driven by the will to succeed, to learn, to improve. Rather than simply accepting what has always been, he injects a fresh, enquiring mind into training, and into the horses themselves. Perhaps

BELOW: *Richard Dunwoody rides Miinnehoma to victory in the 1994 Grand National*

unusually, he analyses his horses somewhat anthropomorphi-cally, trying to reason out their feelings in human terms. He encourages warm relations between lad or lass and horse, and daily doles out ample supplies of mints for the horses.

One day I bumped into a former Pipe girl groom called Clare, who had lived in with him and his wife, Carol. She could not have been more full of praise for her former boss. 'The horses were so well looked after, they lacked for nothing,' she commented, uninvited, and added, 'Martin Pipe himself also has a great sense of humour.'

Martin Pipe trained his first winner, Hit Parade, in 1975, earning just £272 in prize-money. Baron Blakeney was the first horse to establish him on the racing map, when the grey colt

BELOW: *Carvill's Hill, ridden by Peter Scudamore, in the Cheltenham Gold Cup, 1992*

won the 1981 Daily Express Triumph Hurdle at the Cheltenham Festival. By the mid-1980s onwards Pipe was winning races such as the Mackeson Gold Cup at Cheltenham with Beau Ranger, when his seasonal prize-money totalled nearly £250,000; the Welsh National, twice with Bonanza Boy and again with Carvill's Hill; and the Hennessy Gold Cup with Strands of Gold. At the start of the 1990s, when Omerta won both the Kim Muir at Cheltenham and the Irish National, Sabin du Loir had turned to chasing and more big wins came from Chatham and Aquilifer, his seasonal prize-money tally had reached an incredible £950,000+. In the 1999–2000 season, his horses amassed over £1.6 million in win and place money, when they scored 243 wins. He achieved his ambitions of winning the Grand National in 1994 with Miinnehoma, the Champion Hurdles of 1993 with Granville Again and 1997 with his own favourite, Make A Stand. He achieved the big double that year

ABOVE: *Mr Mulligan, ridden by Tony McCoy, eventual winner of the Cheltenham Gold Cup, 1997*

RIGHT: *Richard Dunwoody celebrates his Grand National victory on Miinnehoma in 1994*

when he also won the Cheltenham Gold Cup with Mr Mulligan, both ridden by Tony McCoy.

He won the 'Arkle', the race for two-mile novice chasers, a stepping stone for future Queen Mother Champion Two Mile chasers, in 1997 with Or Royal and in 1998 with Champleve. The equivalent for future Gold Cup prospects, the $3\frac{1}{4}$-mile Royal Sun Alliance, he won in 1991 with Rolling Ball and in 1992 with his future Grand National winner, Miinnehoma.

Martin Pipe rates Arkle the best chaser of all time, and Tony McCoy the greatest jockey, and for 2002 he considers Royal Auclair from his stable a 'very nice prospect for the future'. It is by dint not only of hard work, but also in his enquiring mind and thoroughness that Martin Pipe has shattered so many National Hunt records.

PART THREE

The

Horses

The Hendersons on Lambourn Downs

Mighty Arkle and the Dreaper Days

There will never be his like again. In 250 years of steeplechasing he was and is and surely forever will be the best. Witnessing Arkle was one of life's great privileges. Freak... phenomenon... magnificent... the greatest... superstar.

Arkle in training with Paddy Woods in the saddle, at Tom Dreaper's stables, near Ashbourne, Co. Meath in 1968

The racing authorities in two countries, Ireland and England, changed their handicapping rules to accommodate the might of Arkle: in Ireland by drawing up two separate handicap lists, one with, the other without the top weight; and an 'extended' handicap in England, weights to rise in the absence of the top weight. Proud, regal, imperious, immensely likeable, charismatic. A horse for whom a letter addressed 'Arkle, Ireland' was duly delivered to the stables in the quiet hamlet of Kilsallaghan where he lived in Co. Dublin.

ABOVE: *Anne, Duchess of Westminster, in the paddock with Tom Dreaper after Arkle's Cheltenham Gold Cup victory in 1964*

Arkle was named after a mountain on the Duchess of Westminster's estate in the Scottish Highlands. Once he was in training, he used to spend his summer holidays on the Duchess's farm in Co. Kildare, where she occasionally used to ride him. Once, with only one week between English races, he spent the interval on the Duchess's Cheshire estate at Eaton Hall. Arkle wanted for nothing in life. He had a truly devoted owner who spared no expense; he had a patient wizard of a trainer who was blessed with a delightful and highly efficient wife; he had lads to look after him who were as kind and competent as any. And Arkle

LEFT: *Arkle on his way to the parade at Sandown*

was able to repay them all in the most magical way imaginable.

Nothing too great was expected from Arkle at first. He placed in both his bumpers without winning either, but his work rider, Paddy Woods, recalls that at home he kept on getting better and better, faster and faster, every day. Tom Dreaper's was not a betting stable. He was, however, ahead of his time in his training method, which today is known as interval training. With Tom, it was simply the case that he didn't have wide open heath or downland on which to gallop for miles, so it was a four furlongs canter up a field (no all-weathers then) and a trot back however many times were considered necessary. The horses were given plenty of schooling, which was reflected consistently in how well they jumped on the racecourse.

From the day he made his jumping début a winning one, beating his more fancied stable companion, Arkle swept all before him. Neither fashionably bred nor expensive to buy, Arkle possessed that most important, yet intangible quality in a racehorse: heart, the will to win. And he possessed the ability to match. He was bred in typically Irish fashion by a farming family, the Bakers, who kept a few horses about the place at Malahow and, also following tradition, he was despatched as a three-year-old to the sales. From there, he had the great good fortune to be bought by Anne, Duchess of Westminster, and to be trained by Tom Dreaper, ridden by Pat Taaffe, cared for by the likes of Paddy Woods and his non-riding stable lad, Johnny Lumley, while, always working in the background on his behalf, was Tom Dreaper's wife, Betty.

Some will put Golden Miller, who won five Cheltenham Gold Cups, in the same breath. Prince Regent and Flyingbolt, both trained by Tom Dreaper, were cited by the great man himself as measuring up to Arkle, but not better than him. In thirty-five starts, including three runs on the Flat, Arkle won twenty-seven races and was unplaced once, in a handicap hurdle. He won twenty-two of his twenty-six steeplechases: his first defeat was the result of one of only a few serious jumping errors during his career; he was beaten twice when attempting to give two-and-a-half stone in weight; and, in his final run, he was injured.

Once Arkle made his chasing début a winning one, at no less a place than Cheltenham, he notched seven consecutive steeplechase victories before meeting with his first defeat. This was at the hands of the great Fulke Walwyn-trained Mill House who, as a mere six-year-old, had won the Cheltenham Gold Cup while Arkle was winning the Broadway Chase, now known as the Sun Alliance, the novices' crown at the Festival. In spite of all the hype surrounding Arkle, he was very much the young pretender. The English would not hear of defeat for their big

BELOW: *Arkle and jockey Pat Taaffe, at Tom Dreaper's stables in 1968*

ABOVE: *Arkle, ridden by Pat Taaffe, takes the last fence on the way to winning the Cheltenham Gold Cup, 1964*

horse in the Hennessy Gold Cup, nor did they get it – then. For somewhere out in a murky November mist, Arkle slipped on landing and, although he did not fall, his chance was gone. Pat Taaffe, his great rider, was convinced he would otherwise have won. It was the only time that Mill House ever beat Arkle. In a quirk of racing history, Pat Taaffe had helped to break in the

Irish-bred Mill House and rode him in his first two races for owner Bill Gollings before he travelled to England to join Fulke Walwyn's stable.

Arkle was swift to make amends to his legions of supporters, winning his next seven consecutive chases, including his first Cheltenham Gold Cup. This was in 1964, and Mill House was still expected to win, by the English at least, for he had won not only that Hennessy, but also the King George VI Chase at Kempton on Boxing Day. On an early March day at the Festival, Mill House was favourite, and he set off in front, jumping superbly, to attempt to retain his crown. Arkle could be seen fighting for his head, weaving against Pat Taaffe as he was restrained behind Mill House. By half-way, Arkle was pulling even harder. Their only rivals, Pas Seul ridden by Dave Dick, and King's Nephew, ridden by Stan Mellor, both top combinations, began to drop back. Pas Seul was running in his sixth consecutive Gold Cup and had won it in 1960.

'It's between the big two now,' Peter O'Sullevan's distinctive voice called over the commentary, 'as they turn down the hill to three out.' Mill House was three lengths clear, but two out the two horses were together. Running towards the last, the inimitable Peter O'Sullevan noted, 'And Willie Robinson's gone for his whip, and Pat Taaffe's shaking up Arkle.' Pat Taaffe pressed the button and Arkle cruised by, jumped the last and won by five lengths – a magical experience for any jockey. Afterwards, Fulke Walwyn admitted to being dumbfounded. He simply couldn't understand how Arkle could have improved so much.

The whole of Ireland took Arkle to their hearts, and soon England did, too, for all steeplechasing fans will happily acknowledge and salute a real champion. He became an adored horse on both sides of the water. To use an Irish fan's words, he became 'communal property'.

Shortly after his first Gold Cup, Arkle won the Irish Grand National, traditionally run on Easter Monday at Fairyhouse, a delightfully rural course in Co. Meath, with a steeplechase course two miles round. It is a race the Dreapers, father and son,

Mill House, 1964

made their own. Tom Dreaper won it nine times, starting with Prince Regent in 1942, Royal Approach and Shagreen in the 1950s, and then six successive years from 1960 to 1966, with Olympia, Fortria, Kerforo, Last Link, Arkle, Splash and Flyingbolt. His son, Jim, has won it four times so far: three times with Brown Lad and once with Colebridge. Colebridge was a nephew to Arkle who, apart from winning the Irish National, finished third to Royal Frolic and Brown Lad in the Cheltenham Gold Cup of 1976.

In the season following his first Gold Cup, Arkle turned the tables in the Hennessy in December 1964. On this occasion, he made all the running against his old rival, Mill House, but a week later he suffered his second defeat over fences, by the lightly weighted mare Flying Wild in the Massey Ferguson. It was the only time in his life that he was beaten at Cheltenham.

The 1965 Gold Cup brought Mill House and Arkle together again. Mill House was a horse destined for greatness, who might

have won six Cheltenham Gold Cups, had he not had the misfortune to be foaled in the same year as Arkle. Mill House was great. He had won both his races between the Hennessy and the Gold Cup. By this time, very few horses were taking on the giants, and only four went to post, the other two being Stoney Crossing at 33–1, and 100–1 prospect Caduval. Arkle made all the running, majestically, and try as a good horse like Mill House did, when a notch of rein was let out, Arkle was gone, this time by twenty lengths.

Arkle went on to win the Whitbread Gold Cup at Sandown, the season's final major sponsored handicap, run over 3 miles 5 furlongs. While Cheltenham offers a natural amphitheatre, beneath the spectacular Cleeve Hill, horses nevertheless can seem

BELOW: *Taking the last fence during the 1965 Cheltenham Gold Cup are G.W. Robinson (left) riding Mill House and Pat Taaffe riding Arkle*

ABOVE: *Arkle chests a fence in the 1966 Cheltenham Gold Cup*

quite distant from spectators (certainly before the advent of the big screen), but Sandown offers its own memorable spectacle, especially with the closely sited railway fences, three in quick succession down the back straight. Meet them right on a good stride and there are few greater thrills in steeplechasing. Arkle, carrying 12st 7lb, made almost every yard of the running, jumped extravagantly and dismissed his rivals with ease. His presence had brought record crowds, and they were not disappointed.

Sandown was also the venue for the start of Arkle's new season the following November at the Gallaher Gold Cup (now the Concord Classified Handicap Chase), and it was to be his last duel with Mill House. The big horse, by now in receipt of more than a stone from Arkle, ran with much of his old spirit and glory. It was an incredible race to watch. After a mile, Arkle had pulled his way to the front, ears pricked. The crowd cheered spontaneously, which is most unusual during the middle of a race. But Mill House, ridden by David Nicholson, was jumping with all his old zest, and down those famous railway fences on the last circuit he jumped his way back into the lead. Suddenly

there was real drama in the air. David 'The Duke' Nicholson, who retired as one of the country's top trainers in 1999, believed the big horse had got Arkle at full stretch . . . then, suddenly, there was Arkle ranging alongside again, and still only in third gear. That was the moment, David felt, that the fight finally went out of the big horse, and it is to the greatest credit of his connections, and of the horse himself, that two years later, with Arkle retired, Mill House won the Whitbread, deservedly earning a stupendous reception from the crowds.

Arkle was striding through an eight-race winning sequence at the time of his twenty-length win in the Gallaher, and was unbeaten during the 1965–6 season, taking in another Hennessy Gold Cup, the King George VI Chase, the Leopardstown Chase and his momentous third Gold Cup. It was in the King George that the crack two-mile chaser Dunkirk suffered an internal haemorrhage and fell dead, breaking jockey Bill Rees's thigh. Trained by Peter Cazalet, Dunkirk was a speedy trail-blazer

Golden Miller and Red Rum

Before Arkle came along to dominate the steeplechasing scene so completely, the mantle for greatest steeplechaser had fallen upon Golden Miller, although Easter Hero and Prince Regent both had legitimate claims. Golden Miller's record of five consecutive Cheltenham Gold victories was outstanding.

Red Rum leads at Becher's, second time round, in the 1974
Grand National

LEFT: *Golden Miller, 1936*

trainer fell out with the owner after an abortive attempt on the 1935 Grand National, Golden Miller was trained by Donald Snow and then by Owen Anthony. In his fifty-two races, twenty-eight of which he won, Golden Miller was partnered by no fewer than seventeen jockeys.

His owner, the Hon. Dorothy Paget, was one of the most eccentric in the history of steeplechasing. Vastly wealthy, she bet huge sums, and often demanded food from her servants in the middle of the night. Fulke Walwyn at one time trained thirty-five horses for her, and his widow, Cath, recalls a day when Miss Paget spent literally all day on the telephone to him, from 10am to 6pm. On that occasion, his meals had to be brought to him while the telephone conversation continued. Fulke trained 365 winners for her, including Mont Tremblant, a rich chestnut with broad white blaze, who won the 1953 Gold Cup under Dave Dick, Knock Hard and Phonsie O'Brien having fallen at the second last.

Golden Miller was a fine, upstanding, Irish-bred steeple-chaser, who won the first of his Gold Cups in 1932 at only five years old, ridden by Ted Leader. As the favourite, Grakle, unseated his rider, and the second favourite, Kingsford, fell, not too much notice was taken, but when Golden Miller won again in 1933, it was his fifth consecutive steeplechase victory that season. He then made his first attempt on the National, but fell.

In 1934, Golden Miller won his third Gold Cup by six lengths and went on to win the National in a record time, stamping himself a truly great horse in beating Delaneige and Thomond II, despite mistakes at Becher's both times round. Delaneige led most of the way, but Golden Miller, Forbra and Thomond were close. After the last fence, Golden Miller's jockey, Gerry Wilson, simply let out a notch of rein to win.

The Gold Cup of 1935 was probably the best race of Golden Miller's life, again with Gerry Wilson in the saddle. For this race, Golden Miller had been given a relatively easy preparation, it being Basil Briscoe's mistaken belief that he was unlikely to have much to beat; he was therefore thinking of the Gold Cup only as a prep race

The fact that after the third of them, in 1934, he went on to win that year's Grand National, remains a unique achievement.

Arkle had only one trainer and one principal jockey throughout his career, but Golden Miller was not so lucky. Trained for much of his career by Basil Briscoe, when that

for the National, which in those days was far more valuable.

What followed was one of the great duels in steeplechasing, between Golden Miller and Thomond II. Cheltenham's record crowd witnessed the two horses racing neck and neck over the last mile from the top of the famous hill. The pair remained locked together as they swept round the long bend towards the last two fences, neither horse giving an inch, both fencing superbly at great speed. Even as they jumped the last, there was

RIGHT: *Cheltenham Gold Cup, 1935: Golden Miller with Gerry Wilson up (left) just lead Thomond II*

BELOW: *Red Rum, ridden by Tommy Stack, is cheered as he romps home in the 1977 Grand National*

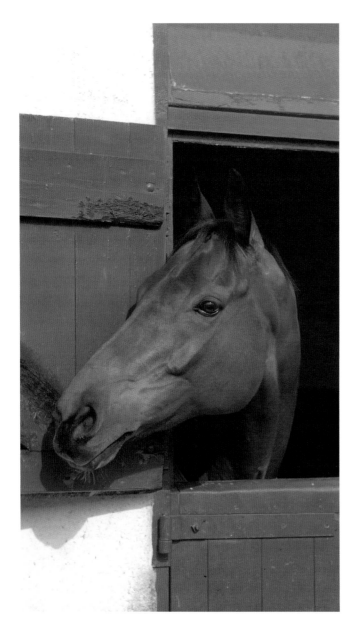

LEFT: *Red Rum*

priced favourite. In spite of his win the previous year, it was a course that he never liked and he wanted nothing to do with it anymore. He won his fifth Gold Cup in 1936 and was trained for the 1937 event, which was abandoned due to the weather. In 1938, at eleven years old and ridden by Frenchie Nicholson, father of David, he finished an honourable second to the younger Morse Code. Golden Miller lived until he was thirty years old. In 1989, a half-size statue of him was erected at Cheltenham, fittingly joining Arkle and Dawn Run there in bronze.

On 18 October 1995, Red Rum was buried alongside the winning line at Aintree. A beautiful gravestone and plaque, in the shape of a horseshoe, was erected. It was done in dignified privacy before the general public was informed of his death. The greatest Grand National hero of all had died at thirty from old age, 'everything just closing down', according to his devoted trainer, Ginger McCain.

For half a decade, Red Rum was the Grand National. To many, he still is. He was a legend in his lifetime. In his tale at Aintree, there is not a single hard-luck story – he even dead-heated there in a five furlong selling race for two-year-olds. His career after that, and before Aintree again entered his life, was chequered, to say the least. Even after a Southport taxi driver, Ginger McCain, persuaded an elderly, wealthy client, Noel Le Mare, to buy the horse for him to train, it was not all plain sailing. The horse turned out to be lame, but being ridden in the sea-water along Southport sands cured that.

Red Rum will be forever remembered for his epic three wins and two seconds from as many runs in the Grand National. He was a supreme athlete, spring-heeled, clever. He was so agile that he could alter course in mid-air to avoid a fallen horse, and he could measure his approach to a fence perfectly, putting in 'a short one' if necessary. This is where his comparatively small size and superb conformation came into play. There is no doubt, also, that he simply loved the challenge of Aintree and rose to

nothing to divide them, and it was only in the last few, uphill, stamina-sapping yards that Golden Miller finally got his head in front. Sadly, Billy Speck, beaten on Thomond II, was killed in a fall on the same course a month later. The record time eclipsed that previously set by Easter Hero, who won in 1929–30, but who was unlucky in the National, straddling the Canal Turn fence and causing a pile-up not far short of Foinavon proportions.

The Grand National of 1935 saw Golden Miller a short-the occasion. Some horses win there, but then say 'no, thank you' on their next visit. The fences on the Grand National course are unique; no other course has fences built either the same way or of such size. As with humans, the big occasion brings out the best in some horses and makes others cringe and shirk away.

When Red Rum won in 1973, he was the usurper of the mighty Crisp. It was another of the great duels in steeplechasing history. Crisp, the huge Australian chaser ridden by Richard Pitman and trained by Fred Winter, made mincemeat of the massive fences. He attacked each one with such enthusiasm, gaining lengths in the air every time, that he set up a lead that looked unassailable, even under top weight of twelve stone. Out of the pack following respectfully behind, there was just one who set sail after him, but even then Red Rum's task looked unachievable. It was only when Crisp's stamina finally gave out on that infamous long run-in that Brian Fletcher was able to coax Red Rum past him.

When Red Rum had to carry twelve stone the following year, 1974, on the good ground he loved, he simply never looked like being beaten, and it was former Gold Cup winner L'Escargot who was runner-up. For the next two years, the hope that there could at last be a triple Grand National winner went unanswered, but only just. In 1975, on the heavy ground he hated, Red Rum was beaten by L'Escargot, the horse he had defeated the previous year. It was more of the same in 1976, when Rag Trade beat him, though not without a struggle. Thus Red Rum had a good record in the race, but so had Manifesto at the turn of the century.

Saturday, 2 April 1977 will forever be etched in steeplechasing annals. It was the day Red Rum became the first, and so far only, horse to win the Grand National three times. He was twelve years old, but when he stepped out on to the Aintree turf he could have been half that age. His self-assurance – and that of his connections – was supreme. Red Rum knew he was king at Aintree. It remains one of the most memorable occasions in 250 years of steeplechasing. With Tommy Stack on his back, along with enough lead to make up the required 11st 8lb, 'Rummy' was

foot perfect, and at the line had put twenty-five lengths between himself and his nearest pursuer, Churchtown Boy.

Red Rum was on the point of running again the next year when a minor set-back prevented him. Then, and for a number of years afterwards, he led the parade of Grand National runners. He also led an extremely active life in retirement, making many public appearances and lapping up the deserved adulation. Red Rum was very special and the choice of burial place for him was totally suitable. His courage and charisma epitomised all that the Grand National stands for.

ABOVE: *Red Rum's grave*

The Snail and the Butterfly: L'Escargot and Papillon, Two Irish Tales

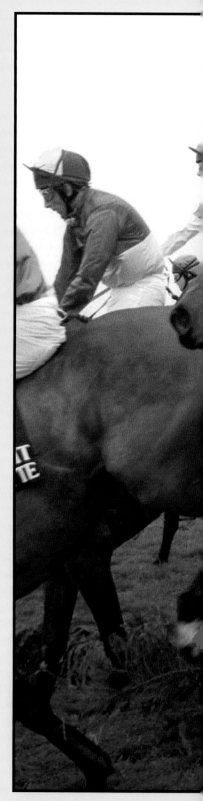

When you meet Tommy Carberry, you know that leprechauns are alive and well. Effervescent, small, wiry, arms waving, he is not only lively but also always smiling. All Irish eyes were smiling the day Bobbyjo won the 1999 Grand National. Bobbyjo was trained by Tommy and ridden by his son, Paul.

Papillon, winner of the 2000 Grand National, Ruby Walsh up

ABOVE: *Bobbyjo, ridden by Paul Carberry (green & yellow cap), eventual winner of the 1999 Grand National*

It was the first Irish victory since L'Escargot's in 1975, when the man in the saddle was none other than Tommy Carberry himself.

Paul Carberry, who has enjoyed a precocious rise up the jockeys' ranks, as well as some bad injuries, shares his father's devil-may-care attitude. This is indelibly linked with prowess and courage in the racing saddle, and Paul loves nothing more than to follow the Ward Union Hunt once or twice a week. It is a pack which hunts carted stag and has a reputation for fast pace and huge jumps. Hunting can cause injuries to a professional jockey, but on the plus side it gives him an enduring eye for a situation and a tight seat when in trouble. Paul Carberry rides very short when racing, even by modern standards, but his innate skill keeps him in the saddle even when his mount makes a monumental blunder.

Part of the whole when considering the family tie with Bobbyjo's Grand National win, is that in the horse's pre-Aintree run, a hurdle race at Down Royal, he was ridden by younger brother Philip Carberry. It was truly a family triumph.

Tommy, five times Irish champion, claims cheerfully that he 'stayed in one piece' during his twenty-one years of National Hunt riding. Some would dispute that statement, given his record of four broken legs, seven broken collarbones, a broken hip and some broken vertebrae. A fall off a two-year-old halted his riding career, leaving Tommy on a respirator for a week.

Tommy always knew he wanted to race and, as soon as he could, he became apprenticed to Jimmy Lenahan on the Curragh, under whose tutelage Tommy twice became champion apprentice on the Flat. He then moved to Dan Moore at Fairyhouse, with whom he remained throughout his career, and with whose delightful daughter, Pamela, the mother of their six children, he has spent the rest of his life.

A quiet start to National Hunt racing was given a timely fillip when Dan Moore gave Tommy the chance to ride in the Gloucestershire Hurdle at the Cheltenham Festival on a horse called Tripacer. It was a never-to-be-forgotten moment and Tommy's face creases in smiles even today as he relives it. His first win over timber! At the Cheltenham Festival! Beating Trelawney and Ross Sea! In style!

At the time, Willie Robinson was stable jockey, but he then

BELOW: *1975 Grand National winner, L'Escargot, with Arthur Moore*

moved to Fulke Walwyn in England. So, at twenty years of age, Tommy Carberry became Dan Moore's stable jockey. Dan Moore had also been a steeplechase jockey and had been beaten a short head in the Grand National on Royal Danieli by the tiny American full horse Battleship, ridden by Bruce Hobbs who, at seventeen years old, was and is still the youngest rider to win the great race. During Tommy Carberry's two decades as a National Hunt jockey, he rode in the National fourteen times, and his record with L'Escargot was third and second to Red Rum, before he finally beat that great horse in 1975.

L'Escargot was one of the best steeplechasers of the 1970s. Apart from winning the Grand National, he was a dual winner of the Cheltenham Gold Cup and was, as I write, the last horse to do so. He shares the distinction with Golden Miller of being the only two horses to achieve the National/Gold Cup double, though with the Miller it was in the same season, 1934. L'Escargot followed up his first bumper and hurdles win by winning the Gloucestershire Hurdle (now called the Supreme Novices') at the Cheltenham Festival. He also won the Meadowbrook Chase at Belmont Park in America, winning a thrilling contest by a head, and earning the vote as Jumper of the Year in the USA.

L'Escargot was owned by American enthusiast, Raymond Guest, who was American Ambassador to Ireland. He achieved his ambition of winning the Derby not once but twice, with Larkspur in 1962 and Sir Ivor in 1968, both trained by Vincent O'Brien, but he set his heart on winning the National, too. Tommy Carberry recalled, 'He came into the yard to look at horses, and picked out Flying Wild, the grey mare who became one of the few horses ever to beat Arkle.' She also attempted to achieve her owner's goal, starting favourite for the National, but fell at the first.

L'Escargot was bought as a youngster and always demonstrated his class and ability. A chestnut by Escart III, a French horse, he was out of an Irish mare, What A Daisy, who was a three-quarter sister to 1958 Grand National winner Mr What. Tommy had his first Grand National ride on Mr What when the horse was thirteen. 'I fell face down in the ditch at Valentine's, where there were two loose horses trotting up and down,' he remembered.

Tommy recalled that L'Escargot was a little bit temperamental. 'I had to tune in to him. You could feel his class, but he had to be enjoying himself. He didn't particularly like leading, but he was the best horse I ever rode.'

There were four blank years for L'Escargot between his last Gold Cup win in 1971 and victory in the 1975 Grand National. He first attempted Aintree in 1972, when he took an instant dislike to the place and was trying to stop at the third, where he was knocked over. The next year, in spite of a run over the

ABOVE: *Red Rum and eventual winner L'Escargot over the last jump of the 1975 Grand National*

Aintree fences in November, Tommy 'didn't think I would get down to Becher's, even in a horsebox'. But, showing he could be adaptable, L'Escargot 'jumped like a buck' and finished third, giving two stone to the winner, in the epic race between Crisp and Red Rum. He was second in 1974, again to Red Rum, when, as he had been trained specifically for the race, Tommy Carberry and Dan Moore had been hopeful of success.

By the 1975 race, L'Escargot's weight had at last, justifiably, come down and he set off in the National carrying 11st 3lb and wearing a hood to 'aid his concentration'. Tommy rode a beautiful race, although the pair almost parted company at the fence after Becher's, the smallest on the course, where the chestnut blundered. By the time they were running to the fourth last fence, Brian Fletcher on board Red Rum could see the Irishman was going better and called over, 'Go on, you've won a minute.'

L'Escargot thoroughly deserved to join the Grand National roll of honour, while Red Rum, of course, went on to put his name in the record books with an unprecedented third win in the National two years later. Tommy added his tribute to Red Rum: 'He went round Aintree like a rabbit – you couldn't knock him down if you tied his legs together. An Aintree horse needs five legs; Red Rum had nine!'

Tommy Carberry's first jumping winner had been at the Cheltenham Festival and, incredibly, his riding career also ended riding a winner there: Brockshee in the Arkle Chase, trained by Arthur Moore, Dan's son and Tommy's brother-in-law. In his most resilient of careers, Tommy had won another Cheltenham Gold Cup, on Jim Dreaper's Ten Up in 1975, and the Irish National for the same trainer on Brown Lad and on Tied Cottage, a horse most unlucky not to have won the Gold Cup. Tied Cottage fell at the last when upsides Alverton, ridden by Jonjo O'Neill, in 1979, and he was first past the post in 1980 only to lose it when a tiny trace of theobromine was found in a dope test. It was traced back to cocoa shells that had been shipped next to the soya beans that were later part of the mix in racehorse cubes. In later years, tiny amounts of such substances fell within the threshold of what was allowed.

ABOVE: *Papillon and Ruby Walsh (green top and cap), in the pack on the first circuit of the 2000 Grand National*

Far from National Hunt racing losing Tommy Carberry when he retired from the saddle, he became a trainer from his home near Ashbourne, Co. Dublin, where the set-up is very much a small, family affair. He has fifty-five acres on which to train his sixteen to eighteen horses. For schooling or all-weather work he takes them to the nearby Fairyhouse racecourse. His wife, Pamela, and children, Thomas in bloodstock shipping, Paul and Philip the jockeys, Mark a carpenter and the youngest two, Nina and Peterjon, both pony racers, all give varying degrees of help around the place, depending on their own work or school. No one deserved to find himself back in the Aintree winner's enclosure more than Tommy Carberry, via Bobbyjo in 1999. Sadly, Bobbyjo had to be put down in 2001, having failed to respond sufficiently to an operation for an injury sustained earlier in the season.

It took Ireland twenty-four years to win the Grand National again after L'Escargot in 1975, but incredibly the Irish won the next year too, and, even more remarkably, it was again a family success, for Ted Walsh trained the 2000 winner, Papillon, and his son, Ruby, rode him.

Ted Walsh is one of Ireland's gentlemen of racing. He was also all-time amateur rider champion, booting home an incredible 600-plus winners (more than any other amateur on either side of the Irish Channel). He has gone on to become a prolific trainer winning with a handful of horses: Papillon (Grand National), Commanche Court (Triumph Hurdle/2000 Irish Grand National) and Rince Ri (two Ericsson Gold Cups), in particular. In addition, Ted is in regular demand as a television commentator and raconteur, and is constantly sought after as an after-dinner speaker. Yet the first thing that strikes one on meeting him is his modesty. Quietly spoken, almost teetotal, he is not one to throw his weight around. Perhaps that is why he is understandably so popular.

An Irishman through and through, Ted spent some early childhood years in the USA. Two of his uncles had settled there and sent back glowing reports: one was a champion jumps trainer, another ran a riding school on Long Island and his son rode several American Grand National winners. It was tempting for the rest of the family to join them and leave behind the life they had known: running the pub in Co. Cork, farming and horse dealing, supplying troop horses, hunting and point-to-pointing. So it was that in the mid-1950s, when Ted was a little nipper, the family sailed on the Mauretania to New York. It was a short-lived adventure. New York winters were cold – very cold. The family rotated around North Carolina, Belmont and Saratoga; it meant many school changes. They were all unhappy and, after only a couple of years, they returned to Ireland and bought a yard in Phoenix Park, Dublin, where it was possible to train in the city centre; Phoenix Park continued as a racecourse

ABOVE: *Hilly Way, ridden by Ted Walsh, winner of the Champion Steeplechase, Cheltenham, 1979*

until 1990, but development was inevitable.

The American experience had some influence, however, for the family found horse dealing with Americans was more lucrative than at the local Irish fairs. In 1960, with Dublin expanding, they bought their current premises at Kill, Co. Kildare; Goffs have since built their sales rings opposite. Ted's father, Ruby, never became a big trainer, because he always concentrated on buying and selling, but in 1966 Ted, then sixteen years old, began race-riding as an amateur. 'I was always going to be too heavy to be a professional, and I was no good for the first few years,' said Ted, in the typically modest fashion of the man who was eleven times Irish amateur champion.

The list of horses that Ted Walsh rode, let alone won on, as an amateur would make many professionals envious. He won bumpers on Brown Lad, Monksfield and Ten Up, and no less than four Cheltenham Festival winners, beginning with Castleruddery in the 1974 Kim Muir. Ted won the race again in 1976 with Prolan. Ten years later, he won the prestigious 'amateurs' Gold Cup', the Foxhunters, on a great hunter called Attitude Adjuster, but it was his win against professionals, in the third of the top three Festival races, that stands out.

In 1979, Ted was booked to ride Mr J. Sweeney's Hilly Way trained by Peter McCreery in Co. Kildare in the National Hunt Two Mile Champion Chase (the Queen Mother prefix was added the following year). There is, of course, great rivalry between the English and Irish at the Festival, and that year was no exception. The English-trained favourite, Dramatist, ridden by Bill Smith, had to take second place behind Hilly Way.

Ted Walsh was as effective over hurdles as he was over fences, and in 1981 he came within one-and-a-half lengths and a neck of landing the hurdling crown, finishing third on Daring Run behind the great Sea Pigeon and Pollardstown in the Champion Hurdle. Daring Run was even better over a longer distance, as he showed when landing Liverpool's Templegate Hurdle (now the Sandeman) twice. In 1981, he beat Pollardstown less than half an hour before Aldaniti's Grand National. It was more of the same in 1982, when he again beat Pollardstown, shortly before Grittar, ridden by amateur Dick Saunders, won the National.

When Ted's father, Ruby, died in 1990, Ted took over the yard, which had been his home for thirty years. He and his wife, Helen, and their three children live on one side of the thirty-box yard, and his mother on the other. Between twenty and twenty-five boxes are filled with horses in training and the remaining few, continuing the family tradition, house horses for sale. It has always been a family establishment, and they have always kept it small and personal; even with his incredible training successes of 1999–2000, he is likely to keep it so, for that is his way of life. He is the first to admit he was fortunate to 'inherit' most of his dozen owners from his father, but then Ted had been part of the overall enterprise for many years. Ted summed it up: 'I would never have taken over the yard when Dad was alive; we got on so well, and I have very good memories.' That family atmosphere is still apparent. Ted and Helen talk with justifiable pride of all their children. At seventeen, their son Ruby was the youngest-ever champion amateur rider, and at nineteen he became the country's youngest-ever champion jockey. Their daughter, Jennifer, is Ruby's agent (he is now freelance), and Ted junior, in 2000, was at college, studying agri-business and playing rugby. At fifteen, Kate is a highly talented rider of whom more may well be heard in the future.

Ted's admiration of Vincent O'Brien has influenced him greatly, never more so than when he ran Papillon in a hurdle race prior to winning the 2000 Grand National. 'Vincent stands out in my life as an absolutely brilliant judge of horseflesh and very talented in all walks. He was a class act. He had the foresight to build Ballydoyle in the early 1950s and brought American thoroughbred pedigrees across. There are so many questions I would like to ask him.

'I asked him once at a party if he would do anything different with a horse before the Grand National. He told me confidence in man and horse was the most important thing, to trust the horse to have the brain to adapt to the fences. He used to school his horses over hurdles prior to running in the National just to give them confidence, something I would never have thought of doing. He got a lot of things right!'

So it was that before contesting the 2000 Martell Grand National, Ted ran Papillon in a nice little confidence-boosting hurdle race. On 8 April 2000, carrying 10st 12lb, Papillon set off at 10–1 in the betting. He and Ruby Walsh gave each other a dream round, only Mely Moss, under Norman Williamson, offered serious opposition in the final mile.

Papillon was bought privately as a four-year-old, unbroken, having passed through the Doncaster Sales ring unsold. Former jockey Brendon Sheridan liked him a lot, so, on his recommendation, the purchase was made. Once he had shown promise at home, he was sold to Pennsylvanian owner Betty Moran. Mrs

Moran, an heiress of the SmithKlein Beecham empire, is an international owner, who had long had horses with Ruby senior and then Ted Walsh, as well as others placed round the world.

Papillon, a bay gelding by Lafontaine, demonstrated his promise. He won a hurdle on his first run at Punchestown, and he followed that with a début chase win at Fairyhouse, in the hands of Charlie Swan. He won again for Norman Williamson and then, at just six years old, cut a hind leg when fourth in the Irish Grand National.

By the 1999–2000 season Ted Walsh nurtured aspirations of running Papillon in the Grand National. He would be nine years old, an ideal age, but his owner, Betty Moran, did not want to run in the National. This is a sentiment in which she is by no means on her own. Anne, Duchess of Westminster, in the 1960s and Richard Burridge in the 1990s were both adamant that their horses would not run in it. Occasionally, one sees a flamboyant horse killed at Aintree, and then one fully sympathises with the owners. Learned and popular opinion is that both Arkle and Desert Orchid could have won the great race 'standing on their heads'. In 1986, the Duchess's colours of yellow, black hoop and tasselled cap, made so famous by Arkle, graced the Grand National winner's enclosure borne by the blinkered character Last Suspect.

In the end, while on holiday in Jamaica, a friend persuaded Betty Moran to allow her lovely horse to take part. Ted was in Dubai when he received the call from Jamaica giving him the go-ahead, and he set about preparing for the big day. Even then, it was only after Mrs Moran had walked the course with Ted that she gave the final OK. 'She had been a victim of hyped-up negative publicity about the race, and had heard of a horse being killed on the first day, without realising that was in a hurdle race. Once she had seen the National course for herself, she realised it was no more daunting than the Maryland Hunt Cup,' Ted recalled.

LEFT: *Ruby Walsh celebrates victory on Papillon in the 2000 Grand National*

If Papillon's preparation progressed smoothly, that of his jockey, Ted's son Ruby, did not. The spring of 2000 brought a fairy-tale ending to what had begun as a nightmarish season for Ruby Walsh. In October of 1999, riding in Czechoslovakia in a race prior to the Pardubice, that country's daunting 'Grand National', a piece of running rail that was sticking out caught Ruby's shin and broke it badly. He was out of action until after Christmas when, riding at home, he had another fall, reopened the injury, and was off the course for another two months.

After being sidelined for five months, Ruby returned to race-riding in March. Less than a month later, he rode victoriously into the hallowed Aintree winner's enclosure. He admits that, but for the second fall, he might have ridden Micko's Dream to win the Thystes Chase earlier in the season – and then he might

BELOW: *Commanche Court*

have opted to ride him in the National, in which Micko's Dream fell at the first fence, instead of Papillon.

Barely a fortnight after the thrills of Aintree, it was the number one spot on home territory for the Walsh family again, in the Irish National at Fairyhouse, with Commanche Court. Ted met Commanche Court's owner, Dermot Desmond, at a Cheltenham party thrown by J.P. MacManus, the owner of Champion Hurdler Istabraq. When Commanche Court was bought in France as a three-year-old, he had already won the Austrian Derby. He was bred in Ireland and foaled at Ballymacoll Stud, Co. Meath, as was Arkle. Ted recalled, 'We didn't know how good he was going to be, but he schooled well at home and the more he jumped, the more he liked it. When he went for the Triumph Hurdle at Cheltenham, it was the first time I'd had a runner of that calibre.' Of all his horses, Ted says simply, 'I hope they keep sound and enthusiastic.'

The Mare and the Grey Horse: Dawn Run and Desert Orchid

The death of Dawn Run in France may not have killed her owner, Charmian Hill, but the venom which was spat upon this remarkable woman may have led to her death from a stroke not very long after. Seldom has there been such an outcry over an owner's decision to run a horse in a particular race.

Dawn Run, Tony Mullins up, leads at Aintree, 1984

The mare should not have run so late in the season, critics said. The owner was being greedy. The jockey (French champion Michel Chirol) was strange to the mare. Dawn Run had done enough and it was unfair to ask her to do more. On and on went the grandstand jockeys and the sofa experts, and even the men in the street. Yet had Dawn Run won, as she surely would have, barring the fall which broke her neck, she would have been hailed the greatest heroine of all time, her already incredible reputation even higher. It made quite a contrast to her Champion Hurdle win of two years previously, when Charmian Hill had been shouldered around the Cheltenham winner's enclosure to an ecstatic crowd rendition of 'For She's a Jolly Good Fellow', or to the jubilant scenes surrounding Dawn Run's Gold Cup win just three months prior to her death.

The biggest charge against Dawn Run's connections (still vehemently expounded fifteen years on) seems to have been that she was running in June, well after most National Hunt horses had begun their holidays, as this was before summer racing was instituted in 1995. But Dawn Run had started her season relatively late, in December, and she had not been overraced. Also she had been successful at this same French meeting two years previously.

But let's remember Dawn Run the racehorse. There are few, if any, mares who can compare with her – and precious few geldings either. She is the only horse of either sex to have won both the Champion Hurdle and the Cheltenham Gold Cup. Other good horses, notably Bula (third), Lanzarote (died) and Night Nurse (second), have tried. She is also the only horse ever to have won the English, Irish and French Champion Hurdle races in the same season. Unique is an especially appropriate word for Dawn Run.

Bred by John Riordan from Rathcormack, Co. Cork, the filly was the sixth foal of her mother, Twilight Slave. At first, they contentedly roamed the meadows near the River Bride, but after two months the foal began scouring badly, developed a high fever and almost died. The vet prepared his client for the worst,

ABOVE: *Charmian Hill, owner of Gold Cup winner Dawn Run, at the presentation ceremony, 1986*

but John Riordan's wife, Prudence, sat up day and night, drip feeding her every three hours, and saved her life.

As a healthy three-year-old, the filly was broken in and sent to the sales, where she was knocked down to an excited Charmian Hill, already dubbed the 'galloping granny' for her steeplechasing exploits, for just 5,600 guineas. Had the filly been a male, there is no doubt she would have been sold for a much greater sum, for she was well bred for chasing and nicely put together, if inevitably still gawky.

It was the diminutive, wiry Charmian who, at the age of sixty-one, rode the mare in her first three bumper races and won the third when, to her disgust, the Irish authorities refused to renew her riding licence on the grounds of her age. No doubt, had this not happened, it would have been extremely difficult for the mare's trainer, Paddy Mullins, to dissuade her from riding at Cheltenham.

Sadly, controversy was never far away from some of Charmian Hill's decisions. When Dawn Run embarked upon her career as a novice, her trainer's son, Tony Mullins, took the ride. But once the big time beckoned, Mrs Hill insisted on a more experienced jockey, so long as he was Irish, and Jonjo O'Neill was engaged. Few will believe that anyone other than Jonjo could have conjured the Cheltenham Gold Cup win out of Dawn Run. Yet it was acknowledged that the mare also went well for her younger rider, who had a style of his own.

When one remembers that Dawn Run was bred and aimed for chasing, her hurdling record was remarkable: she ran in eighteen hurdle races and won thirteen of them. Modest early hurdling successes gradually led to more ambitious events, including running the reigning Champion Hurdler Gaye Brief to a length at Liverpool, the day after winning the novice hurdle there. It gave notice of what might come in her second season, a promise fulfilled as she virtually swept all before her: the Ladbroke at Kempton on Boxing Day, the Irish Champion Hurdle in February, the Champion Hurdle at Cheltenham in March (receiving the new five pound allowance for mares).

For this last race, the mare started odds-on favourite with another exciting novice, Desert Orchid, second favourite out at 7–1. He was the only horse, Mrs Hill once told me, that she had seen jump as fast as her mare. Prior to the Champion Hurdle, he had won six of his seven runs that season and finished second in the other.

At 3.30pm on the afternoon of Tuesday, 13 March 1984,

BELOW: *Dawn Run, ridden by Jonjo O'Neill, ahead of Desert Orchid, goes on to win the Champion Hurdle of 1984*

Waterford was like a ghost town. All its workers were glued to the nearest available television. Dawn Run was a front runner, but so was Desert Orchid. She saw him off after the fourth of the eight flights. Thereafter one challenger after another was despatched, including, as she ran towards the last, her lifelong rival Buck House. But up the run-in a new challenger emerged in outsider Cima. Battling with her trademark tenacity, she held off Jim Old's charge by three-quarters of a length. Desert Orchid finished eleventh, confirming his dislike of Cheltenham, and making his 1989 Gold Cup win there, five years later, even more worthy.

Dawn Run followed up her Champion Hurdle win with a facile victory in the Sandeman at Liverpool, in which she had finished a close second the year before. And then it was off to France.

The hurdles at Autueil are more like mini chase fences in appearance, so it was considered a suitable stepping stone to steeple-chasing. Even more sensibly, since so few English or Irish hurdlers have won the French Champion, she was given a prep race there three weeks before the Champion, where her adaptability saw her cruise to yet another win. An incredulous Paddy Mullins, whose idea it had been to run, exclaimed, 'She's still improving!'

On 22 June, she returned to the well-watered verdant sward. Dawn Run was the make and shape for chasing, and never was this brought home more than when watching her walk to the paddock that day: a big frame, well-developed hindquarters, good bone, even tufts of hair, or 'feathers', on her heels. The contrast with her rivals could not have been greater: they were slim, sleek, small thoroughbreds who would not look out of

BELOW: *Wayward Lad leads from eventual winner Dawn Run (far right) in the 1986 Cheltenham Gold Cup*

ABOVE: *Dawn Run, ridden by Jonjo O'Neill, is led in after their victory in the 1986 Cheltenham Gold Cup*

place flat racing. Dawn Run toyed with them in the race and set up such a clear lead from before the first flight that she never saw another horse throughout the race. She was greeted with rapturous applause, having now captivated French racegoers' hearts as well as those of the Irish and English.

Once more Dawn Run spent the summer in the rambling acres of the Hills' Waterford home, coming in occasionally for a visit from the blacksmith, but mostly left to idle by the river with Charmian Hill's old hunter, brood mare and some young stock. It was not until the following November that Dawn Run saw a racecourse again, in her first steeplechase, a novice event at Navan. Although Dawn Run's jumping was considered suspect in later races, it was faultless on her début. There is a picture of Tony Mullins, her jockey that day, smiling on his way down to the start. It proved well justified, for she fenced well and came

home clear of Dark Ivy and Buck House. She was greeted with euphoria, and a firm belief that she would win the 1985 Cheltenham Gold Cup. Newspapers even headlined her as 'the new Arkle'. Several had tried before to attain the Champion Hurdle/Gold Cup double. Now the Irish believed, almost to a man, that it would be achieved by 'their' mare.

A slight 'niggle', however, kept Dawn Run off the course for thirteen months, so that plan had to be postponed. In 1986, Dawn Run duly won her next two chases in Ireland, but on a January trip to Cheltenham, where the fences were stiffer, she unshipped Tony Mullins. When she ran in the Gold Cup two months later, with Jonjo O'Neill, she had just four steeplechase runs behind her.

Even so, Dawn Run vied for favourite with the current holder Forgive 'N Forget and Combs Ditch. In the race, Run and Skip lived up to his name, bowling along in front until the mare took her rightful place at the head of affairs. A slight mistake at the eighteenth allowed Run and Skip briefly back into the lead, but at the second last Dawn Run led again. Now, however, the more experienced pack was waiting to pounce, and coming into the last fence she was overtaken first by Wayward Lad and then Forgive 'N Forget. To the record number of crowds watching from the stand there was a moment of anticlimax: she had run well, but at best was going to be an honourable third. Most eyes were trained on the two leaders as they set off up that infamous hill. Behind them, Jonjo galvanised the mare as only he knew how. Slowly, inexorably, this greatest pair of tenacious fighters pegged back the leaders and stormed first past the winning post. The crowd erupted. Middle-aged men and women scrambled their way to the winner's enclosure to greet them. Everywhere there were cheers, arms waving, hats wafting, crowds pushing. It was one of the greatest National Hunt feats ever, and it had been achieved in a new record time.

Dawn Run went to Liverpool three weeks later and fell at the first fence. She had met it perfectly, but instead of taking off, she 'missed it out'. The frenzied celebrations that surrounded her at Cheltenham had, it seemed, 'hyped' her up, causing her to lose

ABOVE: *Desert Orchid gallops in riderless after falling during his last race, the King George, Cheltenham, 1991*

concentration. Next, the connections sportingly agreed to a specially arranged match over two miles at Punchestown against Buck House, who had won the Queen Mother Two Mile Champion Chase at the Festival. Clearly, this trip would suit her rival better, but Dawn Run, reunited with Tony Mullins, Jonjo having retired, still won.

Then it was off to France, first for a prep race in which she finished second, and then back for the French Champion. In the race, she went into every fence sharing the lead, but jumped so well that she came out of each with a two-length advantage – until, that is, the fifth from home, when she simply did not reappear. Again, she had 'missed one out' and paid the ultimate penalty by breaking her neck.

Dawn Run was not another Arkle, even her closest connections conceded that, but to have joined Arkle and Golden Miller at Cheltenham in bronze statue form is fully justified. As the only horse to win the Champion Hurdle titles of England, Ireland and France in one season, and as the only horse to win the Champion Hurdle/Gold Cup double, she holds a unique place in steeplechasing's 250-year history.

Boxing Day, 26 December 2000. The runners for the King George VI Steeplechase have paraded and cantered down to the start, but the thousands of pairs of eyes in the packed grandstand are riveted to the finishing stretch in front of them. For there, in his snow-white glory, his only concession to age, is the greatest hero of the historic race striding out in front of his adoring fans. Desert Orchid belies his twenty-two years and storms past the winning post, just as he did to victory a record four times in 1986, 1988, 1989 and 1990. If Dawn Run was the mare of the 1980s – and possibly of the century – then Desert Orchid was the chaser of the late 1980s and early 1990s.

There were several similarities between the two horses. Both were the stuff of fairy-tales. Both were raw-boned, old-fashioned chaser types. Both generated huge followings. And the connections of neither could have predicted the greatness to which they would rise. Because Dawn Run's career was tragically curtailed, while Dessie's continued to meteoric heights, it is often forgotten that on every occasion they met, Dawn Run won, most notably in the 1984 Champion Hurdle, when Dessie finished down the field. Like Dawn Run, Desert Orchid was prone to jumping errors, although he was a spectacular jumper of fences. On his hurdling début, he fell at the last flight, lying

Desert Orchid, Cheltenham, 1991

otherwise have been the case if, say, he had been a bay, but it would have been only a matter of time, for it was his outstanding consistency and flamboyancy over the years that had his fan club swelling annually. He not only jumped spectacularly, but he was also a hard-pulling front-runner whose style always ensured he was noticed by the public.

Desert Orchid was modestly bred by an amateur breeder and could not have been expected to become much more than a point-to-pointer. Both his dam and grandam, bought originally as a hunter by James Burridge, had been very headstrong and impetuous, traits that were passed on to Desert Orchid. When the grandam, Grey Orchid, lost her first foal, she was sent to the nearest, cheapest stallion, which produced Flower Child. Flower Child eventually won two races, and then was put to the stallion Grey Mirage. That mating produced Desert Orchid.

As a youngster growing up in the lush fields of Leicestershire, Desert Orchid frequently got himself into trouble, with scrapes in the field, escapes on to the main road and general tomfoolery. James Burridge's son Richard and a friend, Simon Bullimore, joined in the ownership. As a three-year-old, Dessie was despatched to David Elsworth, a man of deep understanding and astute handling, to be trained at Whitsbury in Hampshire. At first, the future looked more full of problems than of promise. The backward, somewhat quirky youngster appeared to have only one pace, and that was flat out. But in head lad Rodney Boult and stable lass Janice Coyle, the horse – and the trainer – had two superb allies. Between them, Desert Orchid's extremes of energy and enthusiasm were gradually, patiently channelled in the right direction. If he had been mishandled, the steeplechasing world might never have heard of him.

It was in his second season, when furnished up, matured and even stronger, that the racing game fell into place for the grey and, ridden by Colin Brown, the partnership won six of their eight starts, and were unplaced only once, in the Champion

winded for ten minutes, and on his final racecourse appearance, in 'his' race, the King George of 1991, he also fell, but then he managed to steal the limelight as he galloped in riderless, ears pricked, playing to the crowds. Desert Orchid has continued, deservedly, to play to an adoring gallery in his retirement, through many public appearances. Sometimes he is paraded in hand, but when he is ridden, he still likes to give the impression of 'carting' his rider.

The great thing about Desert Orchid above all else was his honesty. Throughout his nine-year career that quality always shone through. The fact that his colour was grey may have made him popular with the general public slightly earlier than might

Hurdle of 1984. The next season, over hurdles, was disappointing, and it was not until he began chasing in November 1985 that Desert Orchid started winning again, scoring in his first four before unseating. He settled into a pattern of winning or placing virtually every time.

Until March 1988, he was ridden by Colin Brown, who then retired. The only exception was when, in the 1986 King George VI Chase, Colin rode David Elsworth's other runner, Combs Ditch. In riding Dessie to his first King George that day, Simon Sherwood could hardly have guessed that he would later go on to ride an unbeaten sequence of nine races aboard the horse, for his next ride did not come until April 1988.

Kempton was founded in the 1870s and was run by the Hyde family for three generations. Its sandy, well-drained soil nearly always results in good ground, and it is a flat, sharp course with tight bends, making it an 'easy' trip to get. The King George VI Steeplechase was founded in 1938 and has always attracted steeplechasers of the very highest class. Because the course is so different from the longer, more undulating track at Cheltenham, it takes an exceptional horse to win both the King George and the Gold Cup, a feat achieved by Cottage Rake, Mill House, Arkle, Captain Christy, Silver Buck, Burrough Hill Lad, Desert Orchid, The Fellow and See More Business. Among outstanding King George winners who never quite won the Gold Cup were Pendil and Wayward Lad.

In 1986, Desert Orchid was David Elsworth's second string, an outsider. There were many observers who questioned David's wisdom in running a proven two-miler in the three-mile contest, to the extent that he began to doubt his own gut feeling. Desert Orchid soon put paid to that. He might never

BELOW: *Desert Orchid statue, Kempton*

have run over the distance before, let alone won, but he set off in the lead, made every yard of the running, jumped superbly and stormed home to the first of his unprecedented four victories in the race. When he was beaten in the race in 1987, it was by Nupsala, a horse whose skilful French trainer, François Doumen, has made it his principal foreign raid.

In 1988, Desert Orchid lined up for the King George unbeaten so far that season and he was odds-on. He did not disappoint his adoring fans, most of whom had come simply to see him rather than to bet. Sweating in eagerness, he galloped straight into the lead. At the water, Vodkatini moved up to join him, and the grey simply outjumped him. Six from home, Desert Orchid saw a long stride and put in a spectacular leap that was stupendous even by his standards. This was spine-tingling Christmas fayre. Vodkatini and Kildimo tried to challenge three out, but at the second last fence Dessie again put in a leap that put the result beyond question. There were plenty of wet eyes in the stands that day.

But it is for his Gold Cup three months later that Desert Orchid is best remembered. He had run at National Hunt racing's headquarters five times before and been beaten five times. If ever he was to bury the bogy, it would surely be this year when, unbeaten in all his races, he was indisputably the country's top steeplechaser.

Then the rain that Desert Orchid so hated fell in such torrents that it lay in pools on the course on the morning of the race. It turned to snow. The fire brigade was called in and started pumping out the water. The chances of Desert Orchid winning looked more and more remote. It was highly debatable whether he should run. He had never won on the course; it was also well known that he hated going left-handed, making him eighteen pounds worse off, said Simon Sherwood, or even 1½ stone, according to owner Richard Burridge. Still the snow fell. The meeting might have to be abandoned. The snow turned to sleet. The improved course drainage did its work, with the aid of the fire brigade. Racing could go ahead. In mid-afternoon, Desert Orchid cantered down to the start with Simon

Sherwood, successful in their previous eight starts, in the saddle. What followed was quite probably the brave grey's most heroic performance of his illustrious career. In spite of so much stacked against him, England's most popular chaser started favourite at odds of 5–2. Also in the betting were Carvill's Hill at 5–1, Ten Plus at 11–2 and The Thinker, winner in 1987, at 15–2.

Because the Gold Cup is contested by the sport's premier, experienced chasers, it is unusual to have many non-finishers, but 1989 was an exception, for no less than eight of the thirteen runners failed to finish in the ground officially described as 'heavy'. Fulke Walwyn's promising Ten Plus led over the first fence, but before the second Dessie was in the lead. Surprisingly, Golden Freeze fell at the sixth, Carvill's Hill at the seventh, an open ditch, and previous winner The Thinker before half-way. Of the remaining runners, a 'pocket handkerchief' could have covered them all. The further they went, the more it was Ten Plus vying for the lead. Yahoo, a renowned mud lover, was there, too. Cavvies Clown and Charter Party were in contention. Five out, Ten Plus was four lengths clear, and he was still leading when he fell at the notorious, slightly downhill fence three out, bringing down Ballyhane. Sadly, Ten Plus's fall proved fatal, for he had broken a hind leg.

It was not all going Desert Orchid's way, although he was beautifully ridden on the inside by Simon Sherwood. Ranging alongside him was the outsider, Yahoo. Now the mud-bespattered horses and jockeys were approaching the last fence. All of them were tiring. Desert Orchid refused to give in. The crowd was roaring. Still Yahoo looked like winning, as Desert Orchid just popped over the last. Simon Sherwood rallied him on the run-in, and straightened him up when he appeared to be leaning on his rival. He was cheered the whole way by Dessie's huge army of supporters, willing the honest horse to win. The wonderful grey strode on to a famous one-and-a-half length victory, and as he passed the post, he pricked his ears. Simon patted him down his neck. It was their ninth consecutive win together, and the twenty-seventh win of Desert Orchid's career

ABOVE: *Desert Orchid, winner of the King George, Cheltenham, 1988*

thus far. Ironically, next time out, Simon's tenth and last ride on Desert Orchid ended in a fall over the Mildmay course at Liverpool, and the winner was Yahoo.

It is surprising for a horse to outlast two jockeys, but on the retirement of Simon Sherwood, Dessie was fortunately teamed up with triple champion elect Richard Dunwoody. Their partnership began with a facile win in a two-horse race at Wincanton, where there is now a race named after him. In their remaining races, from the end of 1989 until 1991, they shared fifteen races with six wins, and finished in the first four on every other occasion bar their last, when, already out of it, Dessie fell in the King George on Boxing Day, 1991.

Worthy of special mention are his magnificent win under twelve stone in the Irish Grand National of 1990, in spite of a monumental blunder at the last fence, and his win under 12st

3lb in the Racing Post Chase at his favourite Kempton in February that year, when an almighty leap at the second last fence put the result beyond dispute. He showed that, like Arkle (but very few others), he was able to give in excess of $2\frac{1}{2}$ stone in a handicap and still win. In fact, the last and thirty-fifth win of his illustrious career was under the burden of 12st 10lb in a race at Sandown in which the second, Nick the Brief, carried 10st 3lb, and the third, Kildimo, 10st 7lb – both of them good class horses.

Five days short of his official thirteenth birthday, Desert Orchid bowed out in front of his army of fans, down but not out, as the picture of him galloping riderless past the stands illustrated so poignantly. It was steeplechasing's great good fortune that Desert Orchid found a trainer, jockeys, owners and carers who were able to bring out the very best in him, not only over a career spanning eight years but, to date, another incredible ten years of public appearances since then. What a star!

The Ugly Duckling: Norton's Coin

National Hunt racing is a great leveller,

but sometimes dreams come true.

While traditionally the Grand National

can throw up a winner at long odds,

it is rare for a rank outsider to win the

Cheltenham Gold Cup, the blue riband

of steeplechasing, as it is contested

at level weights.

Norton's Coin wins the Cheltenham Gold Cup, 1990

As Norton's Coin was led into the parade ring in March 1990, David 'The Duke' Nicholson, former champion jockey and excellent Gloucestershire trainer, was overheard telling Princess Anne, 'That one should be in a dog meat tin.' It was not the first time such a remark had been made about the lop-eared chestnut. He was so ugly as a three-year-old that it was decided not to send him to the sales as 'he would only make meat money'. Instead, he was lent to a riding school on Barry Island, off the Welsh coast for a year.

Sirrell Griffiths is a Carmarthenshire farmer who, like his father before him, trains one or two horses under permit; that is to say, he is not a fully licensed public trainer but is permitted to train for himself, his wife and immediate family. He owned both Norton's Coin's sire, Mount Cassino, and dam, Grove Chance, but sold the mare to a local friend, Percy Thomas, when she was

in foal with Norton's Coin. The dam never raced because she 'swung a leg' and the sire won two one-mile races for Doug Smith, but was hobdayed (an operation to ease a wind impediment) and sold for 700 guineas in 1975. Norton's Coin's great-grandam had been second in both the Oaks (fillies only) and the Two Thousand Guineas (only rarely contested by fillies). Her speed finally was reproduced, it seems, in Norton's Coin – not that anyone could have guessed when he was a youngster. When he was three, he was 'ugly, an odd shape, with huge feet and just nothing about him,' recalled Sirrell, who had no hesitation in turning down his friend's offer of buying him for £500. He was a devil to break, would never school on his own and earned

BELOW: *Sirrell Griffiths, owner of Norton's Coin, is interviewed after the 1990 Gold Cup victory*

ABOVE: *Norton's Coin takes the last fence with Toby Tobias*

plenty of nicknames, none of them complimentary.

After his year at the riding school (how many clients are unaware that they sat on a future Gold Cup winner, one wonders), Norton's Coin was again offered to Sirrell and again he turned down the gawky youngster. The horse was then loaned to another local stable as a hunter and, if he turned out to be any good, would be given a chance in a point-to-point.

His four subsequent runs in Welsh point-to-points hardly set the world alight. Tailed off and pulled up at half-way on his first appearance, the next time out he refused when tired and, of all ironies, baulked Sirrell's own runner in the process. It was on this run that Sirrell noted that the horse who had been conceived on his farm had been nearly a fence behind on the first circuit, but then had 'come like the wind' into contention. A third place next time and finally a modest maiden win led the annual Mackenzie & Selby's form book to comment, 'Won a humble contest readily and may be able to make the transition to Restricted.' Still, it was two years before Sirrell bought him. At six, the horse had had just one run. At seven, in his first hunter chase at Leicester, he finished third in spite of his jockey having broken a rein.

This time, Sirrell really did sit up and take notice. Once more his friend asked his advice on selling the horse. 'Well, I'll give you £500 now,' laughed Sirrell. They did a deal at £5,000, with £200 back 'for luck'. 'I could have sold him on the same night for £15,000, but I couldn't do that to my friend,' Sirrell recalled.

Norton's Coin remained amateur ridden initially, finishing third at Warwick and second at Hereford, beaten half a length, but the next time out, Richard Dunwoody had the ride. The horse was more than a fence in front when he fell at the last at Chepstow and won readily next time at Bangor.

Norton's Coin was on a roll but then, with Dunwoody

unavailable, he finished second in the Cathcart Chase at the Cheltenham Festival, 'flying from nowhere' having been 'out with the washing' on the first circuit. Reunited with Dunwoody, he won again at Newbury, and then went for a valuable race at Cheltenham in April where, an outsider against much better known horses, he 'skated up'. Again, it was his turn of foot at the finish that caught the eye. At the end of the season, he was showing the sort of form that left Sirrell and his wife, Joyce, with dreams of the Cheltenham Gold Cup.

Norton's Coin had a much quieter campaign in 1989–90, and did not reappear until the King George VI Chase at Kempton on Boxing Day. Although Richard Dunwoody wanted to ride him for the season, his first call was to Desert Orchid, so Sirrell Griffiths engaged Graham McCourt. He went to Kempton

BELOW: *Norton's Coin (centre) in the 1990 Cheltenham Gold Cup, with Toby Tobias (right) and Desert Orchid (left)*

without a previous race, never did win a race on a right-handed track, and finished in mid-division. At Newbury, he finished third, but coughed after the race, and a 'scope' revealed a throat infection. Then, in the two-mile Victor Chandler Chase at Ascot carrying ten stone, he was held up and, flying at the end, had too much to make up and finished unplaced. So, with three runs in the season producing just one third place, Norton's Coin took his chance in the Gold Cup. But it was not quite as simple as that.

'Should we? . . . Shouldn't we?'

Sirrell and Joyce debated the decision many times. Then they heard a comment on television from Jenny Pitman. She fancied her horse, Golden Freeze. Norton's Coin had beaten Golden Freeze by a long way at Cheltenham the previous April. If she fancied her horse, why shouldn't they at least enter theirs? Still they debated. He was not the horse this season that he had been last. There was another chase at Cheltenham that might be more

suitable, but they discovered they were too late to enter for that. In the end, Joyce said, 'Well, you've paid the entry fee for the Gold Cup, you might as well go.' Sirrell also noted that there was prize-money down to sixth place, enough to cover his entry fee for the world's most prestigious steeplechase.

'Go on, it's a chance of a lifetime,' Joyce cajoled, whereas their younger son, Martyn, asked, 'What on earth are you going there for?'

Nevertheless, a relief milkman was employed for the day, enabling both Martyn and his brother, Linley, to go. Before then, only one son at a time had ever been able to see Norton's Coin run, while the other remained behind to milk the eighty-four cows. When the day dawned, the whole family set off so early from the West Wales village of Nantgaredig that they arrived at Cheltenham when the entrance gates were still closed. They sat

in a wooden hut, waiting until they could be given their owners' tickets.

Sirrell, being naturally gregarious, tried to talk to the fat man sitting next to him. Sirrell loves to talk, but he found it difficult to engage this particular fellow in conversation. He did elicit that he had a runner in the Gold Cup.

'So have I,' said Sirrell enthusiastically, 'Norton's Coin.'

'Huh,' grunted his neighbour, and turned away from him.

Deflated, Sirrell read the racecard form expert's idea of the likely winner. Underneath the name Norton's Coin was the comment, 'candidate to finish nearer last than first'. Once inside the course, Sirrell bumped into Richard Pitman. Bubbling as

RIGHT: *Norton's Coin is led in after his Gold Cup victory*

ever with enthusiasm, Richard said, 'I was here when your horse won last April, I reckon he should finish in the first three.' It was the sort of tonic that the Griffiths family needed to boost their ebbing confidence.

They went and got some food, and Sirrell ordered a salad, which included spring onions. 'You'd better not eat those,' said his daughter-in-law, Helen, 'suppose you have to accept the Gold Cup from the Queen Mother?' The joke took the pressure off, and before long it was time to go and saddle up their ugly duckling.

Other members of the family and friends went to place a few pounds each way, but Sirrell never bet on his horse. A minibus-load of supporters from the village (more into rugby than racing) had their small wagers too. A family friend, Tony Leighton, went to a rails bookmaker, clutching £60 each way, and asked for a price.

'100–1.'

'But I can get that anywhere,' said Tony, 'make it 200s.'

'Oh, all right, done,' said the bookmaker.

Sirrell, meanwhile, followed Norton's Coin down the walkway that leads out to the course and looked for the gate into the members' lawn. He couldn't find it. All he could see was an ocean of faces, the grandstand packed to the gunwales. 'What am I doing here, with a horse in this?' Sirrell's spirits ebbed. He found his way through to the owners' and trainers' portion of the stand, but couldn't find Joyce or their sons. They were higher up and could see him, but were too far away to call, so Sirrell watched alone.

The tapes were up and the dozen runners for the 1990 Gold Cup were off, led by Ten of Spades for Fulke Walwyn in his last year as a trainer, matching strides with the previous year's winner and odds-on favourite, Desert Orchid. Going out for the final circuit, Norton's Coin was lying in fourth. 'Just stop there, please keep that place,' Sirrell repeated over and over in his mind. They jumped the last open ditch and swung downhill

RIGHT: *Norton's Coin is led in after his Gold Cup victory*

towards the third last, notorious for catching out some horses. The two leaders were tiring, and it was Toby Tobias, ridden by Mark Pitman, who came sweeping through.

Two out, Ten of Spades fell. Norton's Coin was in third place. And Graham McCourt still hadn't moved on him. They were approaching the last fence. 'If he gets a good jump now, he'll win,' thought Sirrell, and in his excitement, with no family to cheer with, he grabbed hold of the shoulders of the man in front of him, one step below. Sirrell 'rode' every inch of the way as his horse flew up the infamous Cheltenham hill, overhauling Toby Tobias a few yards from the line. It was desperately close . . . but Norton's Coin had won. Desert Orchid was third and Cavvies Clown, who had been slow to start, ran on to finish fourth. It was a record time for the race.

The man whose shoulders Sirrell had pumped turned round. 'That's my f***ing neck,' he said. It was the fat man, the owner who he had met that morning in the hut while waiting for their tickets. Sirrell didn't wait to enquire how his horse had done.

When Sirrell, as winning owner, was presented with the Tote Gold Cup, he found the Queen Mother had been well briefed and was easy to talk to. She asked him how many cows he milked, and commented that even when she had had as many as forty horses in training at one time, she had never won the Gold Cup, 'and now you have done it with just two horses.'

The prize-giving was not over. Sirrell also received the trainer's trophy . . . and then £200 as box driver . . . and then another £200 for the groom's prize. 'The only thing he didn't do was ride the horse,' boomed Lord Vestey, chairman of Cheltenham Racecourse, and Graham McCourt walked forward for the jockey's prize.

When the family eventually reached Carmarthen late that night, they found banners across the farm entrance welcoming their hero. Their fields were full of cars. Camera crews filled the yard. And the house itself was full of well-wishers. Soon they ran out of coffee, and drink. At 5.45am two representatives of London papers turned up. Sirrell had been up since 4am the previous day, and had managed to grab a couple of hours sleep. 'Please may we picture you milking a cow?' the photographers asked.

In August 2000, I visited Norton's Coin turned out on the farm in contented retirement. In January 2001, at the age of

twenty and looking a picture, he had a heart attack and died. 'If he'd been trained by one of the acknowledged professionals, he would never have started at that price,' said Sirrell, who added that after the race he received twenty-seven requests from people asking him to train for them. 'Perhaps my one regret is that I didn't take out a licence,' he mused, but then opened his hands around the West Wales countryside, 'but realistically we are just too far away.'

RIGHT: *Sirrell Griffiths and Norton's Coin,*
at home in 2000

Pointers to the Future

We had 'Himself' in Arkle, and 'The Mare' in Dawn Run. Now, at the start of the twenty-first century, and celebrating 250 years of the sport of steeplechasing, we have 'The Lad'.

Limestone Lad, ridden by Shane McGovern, in the Stayers Hurdle, Cheltenham, 2000

ABOVE: *James Bowe*

As a hurdler, Limestone Lad lowered the colours of none other than Istabraq (see pp.53–8), and when he progressed to novice chasing in the year 2000, he won his first four on the trot.

Limestone Lad was meant to be named Fred Flintstone, and the farming family who bred and reared him down in Co. Kilkenny were disappointed when their first choice was turned down. He was a raw, ungainly three-year-old with feet everywhere (mostly on people's toes), and 'more strength than brains', so Fred Flintstone was, the Bowe family felt, the name that suited him. If that remains the biggest disappointment or setback in Limestone Lad's life, then the Bowes admit they will have been very fortunate indeed. The second choice of name has become far more appropriate, for the limestone earth underneath the turf at Gathabawn, Co. Kilkenny, where Limestone Lad is trained and on which he was reared, has, without doubt, helped to develop the good, strong bone with which the horse is blessed.

Like so many Irish farmers, James Bowe bred the odd horse, but mostly hunters and show-jumpers. It was only when he acquired his first thoroughbred mare named Jane Eyre, who bred a succession of winners, that he came into racing at all and took out a permit to train. The second thoroughbred mare he bought was called Kinneagh, and she is the grandam of Limestone Lad.

'We were not in the habit of using expensive sires and we did not see ourselves making a fortune. It was all very low key; farming came first and the horses were sport. Now, with farming in the doldrums, and Limestone Lad's full sister breeding foals for us, it's rather the other way round!'

No one is more aware of the privilege of breeding, owning and training a horse like Limestone Lad than James Bowe, although he prefers not to call it a fairy story. 'It's more to do with common sense and making the right decisions,' he reasons. 'We did not always get it right at first, and didn't realise what we had got, but the horse has helped show us what he needs.' Added to this, the Bowes' son Michael 'lives, sleeps and eats with the horse; he does everything for him.'

The farm at Gathabawn, midway between Dublin and Cork, has a steep hill rising behind it and every day, come rain or shine, be it Christmas Day or any one of a number of saints' days, Limestone Lad is exercised up that hill. The Bowes were not sure, in his youth, whether Limestone Lad would make an eventer or a show-jumper, and he was tried at both. . . . Now, as Ireland's leading novice chaser and hopeful 2002 Cheltenham Gold Cup contender, that experience is standing him in good stead, enabling him to lengthen or shorten a stride when needed.

When we first spoke, in November 2000, James Bowe admitted his horse was still a bit slow at his fences, a trifle 'up and down', 'but,' he said, 'I would rather that with a novice than a flamboyance that can lead to a fall.'

Limestone Lad is a horse who has already captured the hearts of Irish racing folk. They love a hero, and Limestone Lad loves them. A fine upstanding bay, he is totally in love with life and with racing. He has a big personality, which needs channelling in the right direction, and he thrives on a challenge. He has a mentality that is utterly genuine, matched by a big, strong physique and abundant physical soundness. But while proud in public, and happy to play to the gallery, he prefers privacy – 'space' to use a modern idiom – in his own stable. Like many a human star, he would prefer a television company make an appointment to call, rather than turn up at the stable door, cameras whirring, disturbing his private life.

James Bowe has turned down substantial offers for Limestone Lad.

'At first I was tempted,' he admits, 'but the women folk in the family firmly said "no". Now it would be like selling my soul. Whatever happens in the future, we will be glad we kept him. We will always have the videos and the memories.'

In May 2001, Limestone Lad tackled a steeplechase again and jumped well. But while he had been back to hurdling another bright light had stepped on to centre stage. Sackville, owned by Seamus O'Farrell and his trainer Francis Crowley, recorded his eighth steeplechase victory that day at Fairyhouse, and The Lad had to be content with understudy role.

There is no such thing as a racing certainty; money does not buy success; jumping is the name of the game. Never did such age-old sayings ring as true as at the conclusion of the 2000–1 National Hunt season, coincidentally the end of the first quarter millennium of the sport.

Valiantly trying to salvage both English and Irish Festivals that had been ravaged by undreamed of disease and unprecedented rain, racegoers anticipated consolation through specially arranged substitute cards on both sides of the Irish Sea. They were rewarded with good craic, enthusiastic atmosphere and steeplechasing of the highest calibre.

Although they are first-rate courses in their own right, Fairyhouse is not Punchestown and Sandown is not Cheltenham, but both put on Championship races worthy of such accolades. The results proved highly unpredictable. Florida Pearl, twice placed in the Cheltenham Gold Cup, was beaten by Moscow Express in the Powers Label Tote Gold Cup at Fairyhouse. Four days confined to his stable with a bruise contributed to the defeat of Limestone Lad in the Ballymore Properties Champion Stayers Hurdle by Bannow Bay.

The two-day Sandown meeting featured the Whitbread Gold Cup and the new end-of-season presentation of 'The Specials', the National Hunt Championship Awards, when Tony McCoy received his sixth consecutive jockeys' title at only twenty-six years old. In what is normally otherwise a top Flat card featuring Classic trials, there were additional National Hunt races specially designed to make some recompense for the cancellation of Cheltenham. On the first day, the Tote Gold Trophy compensated for the lost Cheltenham Gold Cup, along with a long distance hurdle and a novices' chase.

On the same day, Leopardstown in Ireland featured the Shell Champion Hurdle in which Istabraq was bidding for his twenty-fifth hurdling success. It was widely anticipated that owner J.P. McManus would notch across-the-board victories with mid-season purchase First Gold in the Tote Gold Trophy

LEFT: *Landing Light wins the Championship Hurdle, Sandown, 2001*

and Istabraq in Leopardstown. Both were short odds-on favourites; both had been ante-post favourites for the Cheltenham Gold Cup and Champion Hurdle.

The day started well when the same owner's Barracouda won Sandown's Bonusprint Distance Championship Hurdle; he was beautifully ridden by Thierry Doumen and trained by his father, François. Just over half an hour later, the same combination sent out First Gold. Only Marlborough was seriously backed against him. But at the eleventh fence, hitting it hard and low, First Gold ejected Thierry like a misfired bullet. Far from turning the

LEFT: *Go Ballistic just leads eventual winner Marlborough in the Tote Gold Trophy, Sandown, 2001*

BELOW: *Edredon Bleu, ridden by Tony McCoy, wins by a short head from Fadalko, ridden by Ruby Walsh, in the Championship Steeplechase, Sandown, 2001*

race into a procession, the gallant veteran Go Ballistic made such an effort that it was only by the shortest of margins that Marlborough caught him on the line.

Over in Ireland, an even bigger shock was in store. When Istabraq had fallen at the last flight on the same course at Christmas, he was visibly tired in heavy ground. At the end of April 2001, he was cruising, with the race at his mercy, when he took another crashing fall at the same flight, somersaulting in spine-chilling fashion. It was to collective sighs of relief from both sides of the Irish Sea that he got up in one piece.

And so to Sandown on the Saturday, amid heavy April showers and the presence of the Queen Mother, who unveiled a life-size statue of her heroic 1984 Whitbread winner, Special Cargo. There was the first 'full house' since Desert Orchid's heyday – and he was there, too, galloping past the stands to tremendous applause before the Whitbread Gold Cup.

Two more 'Cheltenham replacement' races took place; the card opened with the Coral Eurobet Championship Hurdle Race, a consolation for Cheltenham's lost Champion Hurdle. Could the four-year-old Doumen-trained and -ridden mare Bilboa overcome both her youth and sex to beat the older geldings? She was up against Nicky Henderson's highly regarded Geos, the Sir Stanley Clarke-owned Barton trained in the north by Tim Easterby and the previous year's Champion Hurdle runner-up, Hors La Loi III. In the event, none of these triumphed; instead Nicky Henderson's second string, Landing Light, in the hands of Richard Johnson, galloped through the mud for owners Mr and Mrs John Poynton.

Steeplechasing at its utmost best was seen in the ladbrokescasino.com Championship Steeplechase – Cheltenham's Queen Mother Two Mile Champion Chase by another name. Fencing over two miles by the country's fastest steeplechasers ridden by the most talented jockeys encapsulates the sport at its most exciting. Tony McCoy was seen at his scintillating best on the title-holder, Edredon Bleu, trained by Henrietta Knight for Jim Lewis. The nine-year-old fenced swiftly and boldly in whippet-like fashion in the heavy ground.

ABOVE: *The Queen Mother unveils a statue of Special Cargo at Sandown, 2001*

Throughout the final mile he remained in front, but it was by only the bravest of short heads that he withstood the sustained challenge of the Paul Nicholls-trained Fadalko, ridden by Ireland's young champion jockey Ruby Walsh for Britain's leading National Hunt owner Robert Ogden. It was possibly as fine a steeplechase as has ever been seen; in many ways, a dead-heat would have been the most just result.

Then it was back to the traditional big race finale with the forty-fifth running of the Whitbread Gold Cup. The top-weighted favourite Beau did his best to make it back-to-back wins, but with the ground and weight against him, he conceded close to home, finishing an admirable fifth to Ad Hoc, who brought swift recompense to the Ogden-Nicholls-Walsh trio.

One more steeplechase, a $2\frac{1}{2}$-mile handicap, remained. The lightning flashed, more rain poured and the remaining Flat races were cancelled. If Red Striker could win, Norman Mason would be leading owner, but a bigger weight than the winner left both horse – and owner – in second place. So, as the good-looking Goguenard jumped into notebooks for the future, the curtain came down on the first 250 years of steeplechasing.

Index

Picture Credits